Genevieve Kingston holds BAs in theatre and performance studies and linguistics from UC Berkeley, and an MFA in acting from Brown University/Trinity Repertory Theater. She is the author of four plays and three one-acts. In May 2021, her essay 'She Put Her Unspent Love in a Cardboard Box' appeared in the *New York Times*'s 'Modern Love' column. *Did I Ever Tell You?* is her first book. She lives with her partner in Brooklyn, New York.

Did I Ever Tell You?

A Memoir

Genevieve Kingston

QUERCUS

First published in Great Britain in 2024 by

QUERCUS

Quercus Editions Ltd
Carmelite House
50 Victoria Embankment
London EC4Y 0DZ

An Hachette UK company

A CIP catalogue record for this book is available
from the British Library

HB ISBN 978 1 52942 410 2
TPB ISBN 978 1 52942 411 9
Ebook ISBN 978 1 52942 412 6

Some names and identifying details have been changed to protect the privacy of individuals.

10 9 8 7 6 5 4 3 2 1

Interior design by Jaime Putorti
Printed and bound in Australia by McPhersons Printing Group

Papers used by Quercus are from well-managed forests and other responsible sources.

To Kristina, Peter, and Jamie.
And to all of you who helped our family through.

When I was three years old, my mother learned she had an aggressive form of breast cancer. Each day she sat for hours at our dining table, her dark hair tied back, surrounded by stacks of paper covered in dense, technical paragraphs. I watched from the kitchen doorway as she researched every available treatment: conventional, alternative, Hail Mary.

Over the next four years she consulted doctors, specialists, homeopaths, and healers. A surgeon cut the cancerous flesh from her body. She adhered to rigid diets and swallowed a mountain of pills. She flooded her body with chemotherapy and carrot juice. She was always looking for a way to survive.

When I was seven, the materials on the dining table began to change. Wrapping paper and ribbons took the place of highlighted pages as her arms worked busily under the dark fuzz of her shorn head. Scissors swished through gift wrap. Paper creased under her fingers. Ribbon was cut to length with one snip. Knots came together with a tiny creak. *Swish, crease, snip, creak.* She had begun assembling two chests of gifts: one for my older brother, Jamie, and one for me.

Into the chests went presents and letters for the milestones of our lives she would miss—driver's licenses, graduations, and every one of our birthdays until the age of thirty. When the chests were full, my father carried them up to our rooms.

Each time I opened the chest, I could inhabit a shared reality, something she'd imagined for us many years earlier. Like a half-remembered scent or the first notes of a familiar song—each time, a tiny glimpse of her.

For years after her death, the pink cardboard chest sat on the floor of my childhood bedroom, and I would open its lid to run my fingers over the rows of neatly wrapped packages, each with a card threaded on thin, curling ribbon. Envelopes thick with typed pages were clearly labeled in my mother's tidy handwriting, an invitation wrapped up in a warning: nothing should be opened before the proper time. Back then, the chest was too heavy for me to lift.

Over the last twenty years, the chest has traveled with me across a continent, moved from state to state and apartment to apartment, always the first thing I found a place for as the moving truck pulled away. It has lived in crawl spaces and in the backs of closets; my instinct is always to protect it. Tuck it away. Every year the chest has grown lighter.

Now only three objects remain inside.

PART ONE

The thing I'd always dreaded happened on a Wednesday night. I was watching Jamie play Warcraft. I liked watching him play computer games; it was how he best tolerated my presence. I could be near him for a long time, watch his dark head bent in concentration, feel his laser-beam focus, smell his comforting boy-smell, and he wouldn't tell me to go away. He was fighting a band of orcs armed with broadswords while crude digital sheep watched the battle from the edges. Jamie delighted me by clicking on a sheep to make it say, "Baa Ram Ewe." Then he clicked on it some more to make it explode. My father came into the room and said that we should come upstairs.

Jamie had unsaved progress and didn't want to stop playing.

"In a minute," he said, swinging at another pixelated orc.

My father gently took his arm. "Come on," he said, in the smooth, rounded vowels of his English accent, slightly faded after more than twenty years in California.

"Will you JUST—?" Jamie twisted his arm away.

After he'd saved the game, Jamie and I followed our father up the gray-carpeted stairs and into our mother's bedroom. I couldn't immediately make sense of what I saw, even though I'd imagined it many times.

She lay where she had for months, in the hospital bed we'd set up in her room. Rain knocked on the windows. Slowly I reached out a hand. I wasn't afraid, but I didn't know a better word. To touch her now was to touch a mystery. She was not cold, but the source of her warmth was gone. What was left was an echo, like the memory of a burn. I looked at Jamie and his face knocked the breath out of me. He knelt by the bed and reached out to touch different parts of her, her leg, her hand, her cheek, as if he was looking for something. He gently drew back one of her eyelids.

"Are you trying to make her look more alive?" I asked.

He shook his head, laid his cheek against her belly, and sobbed. I didn't cry. I'd been crying for years, and now, it seemed, I was dry. A part of me even felt relieved. I was so tired of being afraid.

My father lifted her body and carried it into his bedroom, the one they used to share, so the IVs and other medical equipment could be cleared away. I was surprised by his strength. I'd never seen him carry her when she was alive. Now the women in the family would wash and dress the body. My mother had told me this would happen. It was a ritual she had performed for her mother, and subsequently asked to be done for her. My mother's sister Antoinette, her cousin Sandy, and her friend Sobonfu all beckoned me into the room. At age eleven, included among them, I learned I was a woman.

We took off her oversized T-shirt with the slit cut up the back. By this time, she only wore oversized T-shirts with slits up the back because they were easy to pull on and off without sitting up. This one had a picture of a duck taped to a wall and said *Duck Tape*. She lay naked on the bed, looking not so much like my mother as like a record of what had been done to her. Her left breast puckered with a long horizontal scar, and the nipple was missing. Another long scar ran along her spine from the surgery to repair her broken back. A plastic medicine port made a little hill in the skin of her chest. Her face and body were puffy from steroids. Her hair was short from a final round of chemo, and faint scars showed on her forehead where a metal halo had once been screwed into her skull to treat the cancer that had spread to her brain. She was like a road map, I thought. To where, I didn't know.

Someone filled a bowl with water. We dipped cloths into the bowl and sponged her skin. She was cooler now, losing heat with each minute. I fought the impulse to cover her back up, to lie on top of her, keeping the warmth in a little longer. Already time was moving rapidly. It slipped through my fingers like the water, hard as I tried to make the seconds stretch.

I noticed a mole on her chest, and tried to memorize its exact shape and location. I noticed the light stretchmarks sketched around her breasts and belly, mementos of two pregnancies. I noticed the delicate ridges on her fingernails, and the deep lines of her palms, and wished I could read them. Maybe they told a story with a different ending. The glowing green display of the CD alarm clock caught my eye: it was 10 p.m. on a Wednesday. We should have been watching *Star Trek*.

My mother had been a skinny, dark-haired teenager when the original *Star Trek* series first aired. Like many girls her age, I imagine she harbored a crush on Captain Kirk, played by a young William Shatner. When the show's sequel, *The Next Generation*, began airing in the late eighties, our family watched religiously. From as far back as my memory goes, the four of us would pile onto the battered brown faux-leather couch, as the words "Space, the final frontier," uttered in Patrick Stewart's Royal Shakespeare Company baritone, reverberated from our black boulder of a television. These words signaled that, for the next hour, my family would surround me, all safe. My favorite character was the ship's counselor, Deanna Troi, and I dreamed that one day my straight, dirty-blond bangs would transform into her gorgeous mass of midnight curls.

For me, the show also opened up a new concept of time. In *Star Trek*, time was something that could be altered and molded and re-worked. If the *Enterprise* exploded, I knew, someone would have to go back in time to fix it. A thousand times, in my imagination, I sank through layers of time to the moment when my mother's cancer began, and plucked it out before it could take root.

After *The Next Generation* aired its final episode, my mother began allowing me to stay up late with her on Wednesday nights to watch *Star Trek: Voyager*. My adoration for Voyager's commanding officer, Kathryn Janeway, far eclipsed what I'd felt for Deanna Troi. Janeway's starship had been lost in a far-flung quadrant of the galaxy, stranding her crew thousands of light-years from home. *Voyager* was a saga of homesickness, and I'd been homesick for as long as I could remember, not simply for a place or a person, but for a world in which my mother wasn't going to die. And Captain Janeway had straight, dirty-blond hair.

Wednesday after Wednesday, my mother and I watched the crew of the USS *Voyager* hold their own in the Delta Quadrant, and knock out another obstacle in a journey that was projected to take more than seventy years. At first, my mother and I watched while sitting on the couch together. Then we watched side by side in her hospital bed. And finally, when she was no longer awake, I watched from her bedside and held her hand. She would miss the final episode by three months.

And so, at 10 p.m. on Wednesday, February 7, 2001, I was washing my mother's body, and wishing I could turn on *Star Trek*. I looked into the faces of the other women, and I knew that I'd never be able to explain to them why I wanted to switch on the TV. Why I wanted to sit with my mother one more time as the opening credits sent the lights of novas and warp engines across our faces. Why, especially in that moment, I needed to know that some things were still the same. Why I craved another understanding of time. I'd never be able to explain to them that we'd all been on a journey together for years, me and my mother and Captain Janeway and *Voyager*, a journey home that we knew might take our whole lives.

Ten days later I turned twelve.

I woke early to a quiet house and, like the previous ten mornings, wondered if I'd dreamed it. Maybe, if I opened my door and walked down the gray-carpeted hall to the room next to mine, I'd see her lying there, IVs dripping, machines humming, breath stirring the air around her sleep. That morning, like the last ten mornings, I lay in bed until the wondering faded away. This was real. This would be real for the rest of my life. This would be real after I died.

I swung my bare legs out of bed. I was wearing one of the night-gowns she'd made for me. Every summer she made three: two long-sleeved, one short-sleeved, two cotton, one flannel. Every year she'd make them one size larger, carefully lining up the front pockets so they blended perfectly into the pattern. This one was too small, because for the last two years she couldn't see well enough to do the sewing, and she couldn't sit up to use the machine. It dug in under my arms.

My mother and I shared a birthday, and any other year I would have run down the hall and crawled into her bed. My father would have brought us hot chocolate or a bunch of flowers, and called us "the birthday girls." My mother would have squeezed me and said, as she did every year, "The best birthday present I ever got." Instead, I stayed in my bedroom, delaying the moment I would have to open my door and find her gone.

For months the cardboard chest had sat on the floor of my bedroom, and I had tried to ignore it. During those months, the chest had represented a future I'd hoped would never come. Now I moved slowly from the bed and knelt beside it. I drew the latches back one at a time, making the moment last. When I lifted the lid, the first thing I saw was a large black spiral-bound sketchbook with two red pears on the cover. My breath came faster as I pulled it out and opened it to the first page.

Dearest Gwenny

A record of letters and keepsakes put by to acknowledge and celebrate significant life events. I've made this record for you just in case something happens to the letters and keepsakes themselves. The pen I used to write this record I also give to you and may it give you pleasure.

Love, Mommy

Clipped to the binding was a green and gold fountain pen, the kind that used wet ink. I pulled it free, feeling its surprising weight in my hand. Tears blurred the words on the page in front of me. My mother had shown me the sketchbook years before, and, like the chest, I'd pushed it to the back of my mind, another tool I didn't want to learn how to use. I measured its thickness in my fingers, and pressed it to my ribs, hungry for the words promised inside.

Beneath the sketchbook, the chest's contents came almost to the lip. Boxes of different shapes and sizes fitted together in a three-dimensional puzzle. Taped inside the domed lid, a thin sheet of graph paper catalogued the chest's full contents. I ran my finger down the list. Birthdays gave way to graduations to marriage to children. Beside each item, a checkmark showed it was present, accounted for.

I searched the top layer of packages until I found the one marked *Gwenny's 12th Birthday*. It was a cardboard box patterned with sea-shells, tied with pink, curling ribbon. Holding it in my hand, I felt the first sharp twinge of curiosity to see what my mother had chosen for me. I untied the ribbon and opened the box.

Inside I found a small brass ring in the shape of a flower with a tiny amethyst set into the center. Amethyst was our birthstone. The back of the card said, *Happy Birthday darling girl! pg. 8*, and I flipped through the creamy white pages of the sketchbook. On the top of page 8 was a photograph of the ring, and beneath it my mother had written a handful of sentences.

Dear Gwenny,

This was my second birthstone ring. I always wanted a birth-stone ring when I was a little girl and begged Granny Liz for one. Eventually, she relented and we selected a pretty little ring at a local jewelry shop. I loved it more than I can say. One day, when

I went swimming at the Terrace Plunge, I wrapped it up in my
towel for safe keeping. When I came back from swimming, it was
gone. I was devastated. G. Liz and I found this replacement at
Cost Plus in San Francisco. I hope you like it too.
　xox Mommy

The ring fit my right index finger. I slid it on, and tried to imagine my mother slipping the same ring onto her finger for the first time. I tried to hold her in my mind like that, a little girl, guilty over losing the old ring, grateful for the new one. More than three decades separated that moment from this. I was born the morning my mother turned thirty-seven. On this day, she would have been forty-nine. I held the sketchbook open on my lap, and traced the marks from her pen. Her words, written to bridge the gap between us, cut through space and time. I read them again and again.

I don't remember learning my mother was sick. My memory clicks on sometime after the day she came back from the doctor with the news that the lump in her breast wasn't a clogged milk duct left over from breastfeeding me. I don't remember the blue and white house where we were living when it happened, apart from the blurry outline of a splintery wooden jungle gym and bedroom wallpaper with ducks around the top. Somewhere in that house there must have been a tiny black-and-white puppy, a ranch runt with a strong herding instinct and two different-colored eyes. But Tippy comes to me only as a full-grown lady dog, the white stripe on her nose covered in dirt, her mouth full of rubber tubing ripped from my father's sprinkler system, tail a-wag. The puppy, like the diagnosis, is lost to the primordial ooze of *before*.

The house I do remember was a pale-gray two-story hiding its face behind a curtain of purple wisteria. It had a generous porch set with white wicker furniture, and a brass mailbox next to the front door. A few doors to the left stood the grand mansion where *Pollyanna* was filmed in 1960, and in which my grandmother had made an appearance as an extra. When we moved in, Granny Liz still lived a block and a half down the road. My mother, like a sea turtle, returned to the place where she grew up to raise her own family. Our new house was much larger than the one we'd left, with four bedrooms, a two-car garage, and a swimming pool in the backyard, financed by a recent inheritance on my mother's side. We moved in soon after her cancer diagnosis, on my third Fourth of July.

My mother painted the four bedrooms a shade like watercolor sky. I was going through a princess phase, and my father thrilled me by hooking a tent of gauzy mosquito netting above my polished-pine twin, which made me feel exactly like Disney's Jasmine, minus the tiger.

My brother and I shared a bathroom and a wall. Jamie's room would come to hold an imposing collection of Legos, along with shelves of Dungeons & Dragons miniatures at various stages of painting. I was jealous of his imaginary worlds. He could spend hours alone in them, insulated from the anxiety about my mother's health that was already dividing and multiplying inside our house. My own games of make-believe were haphazard, vague chapters of "my bed is a pirate ship" or "mixing magic potions out of dirt." I was allowed provisional access to his rarefied multiverse. He didn't mind if I watched while he painted or read, as long as I didn't say anything. I craved his attention like air, and a single word or glance, grudgingly bestowed, could sustain me for hour after blissful hour. He called me Gwenny, after Queen Guinevere from his favorite movie, *Camelot*; and even though I was Genevieve on my birth certificate, his name stuck.

The street out front was a wide avenue lined with magnolias, maples, and ginkgoes. One end led to the main road into downtown Santa Rosa, the other to the local cemetery. Each Fourth of July, for as long as they lived there together, my parents threw a block party on the street in front of our house. My English expat father loved the American Independence Day, but insisted on flying a Union Jack flag alongside the Stars and Stripes.

It was still legal to set off your own fireworks, and all down the street families sat in the road making tiny, bright explosions. The air smelled sharp and potent, like the head of a match. Uncle Jonathan (called Uncle Q) was the youngest of my mother's three brothers. He always arrived while it was still light, carrying bags of his home-made pyrotechnics. Matchstick thin himself, he would save the casings from last year's fireworks, and pack them with the explosives from Piccolo Petes so that they went off like artillery fire when you were least expecting it. He'd always had a soft spot for combustibles. As a teenager, he'd been rumored to blow up mailboxes with cherry bombs along that very street.

I can picture our dog Tippy, skittish from the fireworks, lying unusually still, a taut black-and-white stripe on the ground. As the sun set, Jamie and my older cousins would each be allowed to light a sparkler. They'd run and twirl and write their names, burning bright momentary sketches into the gathering dark. Granny Liz, having walked the two hundred paces down the street from her house, would sit straight-backed in a folding chair, a tartan blanket covering her lap and a pair of oversized spectacles (she called them "spectaculars") sticking their curved arms back into her short, silver-threaded hair. My mother's sister Antoinette would be sitting nearby.

My father, in khaki shorts and tall white socks, would be lighting the barbecue, a smoking tower of newspaper collapsing toward the coals, a row of chicken quarters lined up for charring. My mother would ready the hose in case either the barbecue or the Frankenstein-ed fireworks got out of hand. She'd be alert, taut like Tippy, allowing the rest of us our fun while preparing, always, for disaster.

The first steps in my mother's treatment were a single mastectomy to remove the entire right breast along with the tumor, and a reconstruction to fill the empty space it left behind. A long pink scar replaced her nipple, like a mouth with lips sucked in, sealing off, we hoped, the threat inside. At first, my parents would only say that she was sick. Later they explained that, even though her surgeons had been thorough, her age (only forty) and the aggressiveness of the cancer meant that it would likely come back. Her doctors recommended radiation, then chemotherapy.

For weeks after my mother came home from the hospital, I refused to leave her side. I followed her from room to room, even into the bathroom, afraid she might vanish in the time it took me to blink. During those weeks, I watched the long oval of our dining table disappear under piles of paper. Each day she'd sit for hours, highlighting journal articles and thumbing through stacks of printed pages.

"It was one of the most difficult decisions of my life," she'd say a few years later, looking into the lens of a camera as she recorded a video message for my brother and me, "what I was going to do to fight the cancer. I spent six weeks reading and researching and talking and praying. I made the choice to have surgery, but not to do the conventional treatments that were recommended to me. I felt that I would not be able to withstand the toxicity of the treatment. I felt that it would make me too sick and I wouldn't survive it. I don't know whether that was true or not; it is what my intuition told me was true."

Instead, she sought out a private, alternative treatment program known as the Gonzalez Protocol.

Dr. Gonzalez told my mother a cure was possible, but only if she had no outside clinical intervention of any kind: no tests, no scans. Any other doctors she visited would have to work within the parameters he set. While on his program she followed a strict vegetarian diet, took up to a hundred pills every day, and gave herself twice-daily coffee enemas. She also bought a General Electric Champion juicer, a massive thing of beige plastic and enamel that claimed an entire countertop. She ran a whole bag of carrots through the Champion daily, and drank full glasses of the frothy orange glop.

"It's anticarcinogenic."

I asked her what that meant.

"It prevents cancer," she said, "and carotene also helps you see in the dark."

I tried a few sips of the orange sludge. I thought it tasted like tree bark. Later I went outside to test my night vision, but nothing seemed different. I suspected this was just another grown-up ploy to push vegetables.

My mother drank carrot juice until her hands and face turned orange. The next year, in preschool when we scribbled pictures of our families, all the other white kids would use the orange crayon for skin.

"But my mom's really orange," I'd announce, "so it's realistic."

It was the nineties, and my parents were true believers in homeopathy and natural remedies. They owned and operated a small beverage company, an early pioneer in the use of nutritional additives. It was called Mrs. Wiggles Rocket Juice and their slogan was "Nutrition for your mission." Jamie and I, together with Uncle Q's daughters, Jessie and Tori, haunted the big warehouse where juices like Gingko Think and Spirulina Smoothie were mixed, bottled, labeled, and packed. The four of us would compete to see who could stay longest inside the walk-in refrigerator, our teeth chattering, our fingertips slowly turning blue. There was one glorious room filled with heavy cardboard boxes stacked in enormous mountains that we would scale to the top, or rearrange into elaborate fortresses. The air at the juice company smelled like a rainforest: damp and sweet and alive. In my father's office, a long board hung on the wall with every Rocket Juice label they'd ever produced. Each one had a tiny rocket ship hidden somewhere in the design, and I stared at them until I could find every single one.

At home in our kitchen, everything was organic. We didn't shop at Safeway, like my friends' families. Instead, Jamie and I trailed our mother through the narrow aisles of Community Market—the local independent health food store—which sold things like lentils in bulk and smelled of beeswax candles and vitamin powder. For mild ailments, we visited homeopathic doctors for brown glass vials of arsenic and opium, diluted and compressed into tiny white sugar pills we dissolved under our tongues. No one in our house drank, smoked, or ate processed foods. We exercised. We flossed. We were a poster family for healthy living; except one of us was sick.

If I close my eyes, I can still see my mother sitting at our dining room table, her eyes down, a mug of lemongrass tea steaming beside her. She leans forward on brown, freckled arms, poring over the results of clinical trials, snipping articles from magazines. More than anything in the world, I want to throw my arms around the woman at the table, and whisper what I know about the future into her ear: that Dr. Gonzalez does not have the answers she's looking for. That despite all her intelligence, her effort, her instincts, she is putting her trust in the wrong person.

When I was four, we got a parakeet named Davey who was yellow and green with little blue spots on his cheeks. He had a white domed cage with a chalky cuttlebone and a bell hanging from a piece of yarn. He also had a mirror, but we had to remove it when he started challenging his reflection to wing-flapping contests that shook the whole countertop. His primary feathers stayed clipped down close to the wing, so we left his little white door wedged open, and he could flutter around the house, landing on fingers, shoulders, heads.

Davey spoke in tiny squeaks and chirps and head tilts. I learned to mimic them exactly so I could repeat back whatever he said to me. He spoke and I repeated, over and over, him training me, instead of the other way around. I never knew what we were saying, but I was sure it was something secret and beautiful. He would take my finger gently in his beak and turn his head to look up at me with eyes that were the size and color of black sesame seeds. Occasionally Jamie would interrupt our conversations to say cheerfully, "Chirp chirp, little twerp!" and then wander away again.

At noon, when both hands pointed to the artichoke at the top of our kitchen clock (which had vegetables instead of numbers around the edge), I would barrel in the door from preschool, and Davey would sing out a greeting. His chirps signaled that I had survived another morning away from home. Five days a week, my mother dropped me off at First Presbyterian Preschool, a block and a half from our house, and every morning I screamed, sobbed, and begged her not to leave me there. I clung to her with arms, legs, and teeth.

"Please!" I'd shriek after her retreating back, restrained by the strong arms of a teacher. "Please come back!"

Separating from my mother felt like walking around without my skin. I knew that her life was in danger, and I was terrified to spend even a few hours away from home. What if she died while I was gone? I didn't trust anyone else to keep her safe.

At school, I wandered from room to room, occasionally playing, mostly staring at the big black clocks that hung over every door. When the school day ended, I'd rush outside, climb to the top of the jungle gym, and stare over the playground fence toward my front gate, focusing all my energy on making my mother appear beyond it.

One summer Davey developed a mass on his leg and we took him to the vet to have it removed.

"He has to have surgery," my father said in the car.

My mother joked, "Do you think they'll put a tiny gas mask over his beak?"

I imagined him gowned and sedated on a tiny operating table while masked figures hovered over him with toothpicks and tweezers. He came home without the lump, but the cancer was already inside his hollow bones.

Davey had always slept in my room, but after the surgery my mother moved him into hers because I sometimes forgot to take the bath towel off his cage in the mornings, leaving him in perpetual night. Suddenly he needed things I couldn't give him, like medicine and sympathy. I knew I should feel sad about my bird's bones, but the bones were invisible, and so I couldn't manage to feel anything about them at all. Like my mother, Davey didn't look sick. He still had all his bright feathers and the same inquisitive look in his sesame eyes. He would still land on the top of my head and poop and fly away, making a sound like high, whistling laughter.

If cancer was invisible, that meant anyone could have it. I imagined it creeping from person to person like head lice. They talked a lot about head lice at my school.

"No," my mother said, "you can't catch cancer from Davey, or from me. It's just something that goes wrong inside."

One morning my mother came into my room with something in her hands, and pushed back the princess mosquito netting to sit on the edge of my bed.

"Last night Davey seemed very anxious and he was flying all around his cage. So I took him out and I just held him against my heartbeat, and that seemed to calm him down. We stayed like that for a couple hours, and then I couldn't feel his heart against mine anymore, and I knew he'd died."

Looking at the bundle in my mother's hands, I sensed what was about to happen and my whole body tensed against it. I didn't want to see. I half-closed my eyes, as if that would let in only part of the truth, but she folded back the cloth and there he was, between the dark rims of my eyelids, all yellow and green and still.

"You can touch him," she said.

Very slowly, I put out a stiff finger and stroked the soft speckled feathers.

On Davey, death looked ancient. Reptilian hoods covered both his bright eyes and I noticed, as if for the first time, his scaled legs and curved claws. He looked smaller and a little alien, like sixty million years of evolution asleep in a cloth in a hand on my bed. For a long time my mother sat there, letting me cry, holding that ending in her palm.

We buried Davey in a formal ceremony in the front yard. We shoveled his grave beneath a box hedge, and marked it with a little wooden cross. I sprinkled sprigs of daphne, pulled from bushes in the back garden, on the turned earth before we lowered Davey in. Around him we laid fronds of millet and a cuttlebone: his favorite things. I cried, and everyone said a few words, and all the time I felt my mother's eyes on me.

Each time Davey had molted over the years, my mother had collected the fallen feathers from the bottom of the cage and put them in a clear plastic box full of little square compartments, the same kind she kept her many pills in. There were long graceful primary feathers with their tips cut at a sharp angle; there were downy chest feathers of lemon-butter yellow; and in the smallest compartment she kept her favorites: the tiny cheek feathers with their little dots of blue. She said she might use them in an art project one day.

My mother had always held on to things. The drawers and cupboards of our house were full of shells and stones collected on long walks, old letters and birthday cards, photographs piled into shoeboxes. Even things like wrapping paper and plastic yogurt containers were kept and reused. But as her illness progressed, I read new meaning into her saving. Over the coming years, I considered every leaf or flower she picked up and pressed between the pages of a book, every piece of old ribbon she rolled neatly into a ball, every stray button she placed in her sewing basket to be a good omen. To me, each one signaled her belief that she still had a future.

The theme for my fifth birthday party, the first one I can remember, was *Alice in Wonderland*. I still have one of the enormous invitations my mother made out of construction paper to look like the Mad Hatter's gray topper. Inside, a cast list assigned every guest a character. The children were the Cheshire Cat, or the Caterpillar, or Tweedledee. The grown-ups were a pack of playing cards. I, of course, was Alice.

My parents recruited Granny Liz to drape long reams of butcher paper across our front porch, and paint them to look like the entrance of a rabbit hole. My father, as the White Rabbit, rented a full bunny suit from the local costume shop—Disguise the Limit. My mother constructed a set of flamingo croquet mallets from plastic golf clubs that she stuck into the legs of hot-pink nylon tights. She gave them round heads and soft little bodies of quilt batting, separated by long necks. She finished the flock with felt feet and beaks and rolling googly eyes. They lay ready on the back deck, next to a brace of Styrofoam balls wrapped in faux fur hedgehog bristles. On the day of the party, I stood on the front porch in my blue dress and pinafore, waiting for everyone to arrive.

The guests came in face paint, felt ears, and furry tails, and we gathered in the dining room for cake and milk. My father had printed out the script from the scene in the Disney film where Alice stumbles upon a mad tea party, and my mother had constructed a giant pocket watch out of cardboard and covered it with gold foil. While Jamie (the March Hare) and our mother's friend Nancy (the Mad Hatter) read their lines, we acted out the sequence in which the guests fill the White Rabbit's watch with butter, then tea, then jam. Afterward we played croquet, using our flamingos to knock the hedgehogs through white wickets driven into the lawn.

My mother had dressed as the Duchess's cook, a tall chef's toque on her shiny dark hair and a white apron around her waist. She moved among us through the backyard, occasionally shouting, "More pepper!" as she rattled confetti over someone's head from a giant shaker made from an empty coffee can. She was forty-two that day. She'd tell me later she'd been looking forward to her forties. She'd seen the new decade as a chance to shed old grudges and expectations, and begin a more authentic chapter.

My memory has both preserved and polished the day of the party, buffing away any rough edges. On that day, it seemed possible that my mother's treatments would work. She looked well and strong, standing on the back deck in her white cap and apron, surveying the results of her labors. She had planned and executed the birthday party the same way she managed her complex cancer treatments, the same way she did everything: meticulously, tirelessly, in exquisite and excruciating detail.

Another year, she and my father would enlist family members to paint life-sized illustrations of Dorothy, the Tin Man, the Scarecrow, and the Cowardly Lion onto huge pieces of cardboard—positioning them around the house for Jamie's *Wizard of Oz* party. For his *Teenage Mutant Ninja Turtles* party, they made and distributed fabric ninja masks, and our father, dressed as Shredder, staged the kidnapping of our cousin Jessie. For my *Under the Sea* party, my mother spent days folding a school of origami fish to swim through tissue paper seaweed across the ceiling of our dining room. In the midst of all the terror over my mother's illness, the parties were something to look forward to. They became like huge village festivals. Friends, family, and neighbors were all roped in to help execute these spectacular visions, and for the weeks it took my mother and father to prepare all this pageantry, they seemed happy.

After each party, my parents left the decorations in place, and they accumulated on top of each other until our house was like a museum of childhood fantasies. For over a decade the scenes from *The Wizard of Oz* lined the walls of the house. The fish continued to swim across the dining room ceiling. The huge playing cards stood lashed to the banisters like empty suits of armor, and an honor guard of shocking-pink flamingos, stationed around the front hall, watched over us with their googly eyes from under a thickening layer of dust.

My parents, Peter and Kristina, met at a party in San Francisco in 1981, and married two years later in that same city. He was a chartered accountant and she had just graduated from business school. My father had left England several years earlier, but still said things like "jolly good" and "bloody hell" and "crikey." He was handsome in a James Dean–meets–Hugh Laurie way, with blue eyes and strawberry-blond hair, both of which he passed on to me. He always carried a handkerchief in his pocket, and tied knots in it to remind himself of things he'd forget anyway. His name was Peter Kingston, but my mother called him Peter Pan.

My father could turn anything into a game. The smallest bit of sloping grass in front of a church or a bank was an opportunity to play "The Grand Old Duke of York"——marching us up to the top of the hill and marching us down again. He loved shortcuts. Our first, blue-and-white house stood across the street from an elementary school that padlocked its playground fence each night. My father took a pair of bolt cutters to the chain that held the gate closed and added his own padlock next to the school's, so he could open it whenever we wanted to play there. Periodically the school replaced the chain, and he'd buy another lock. For several years I had a friend called Travis, whose house sat directly behind ours. My father sawed a rectangle out of our back fence, and fitted the cut-out piece with hinges and a metal latch. Then he went over to Travis's house and cut a hole in his fence as well. The passage connecting these two doors ran through a small gap between our neighbors' back fences, and was heavily overgrown with ivy and infested with wolf spiders. Now and then my father would go through it with a machete, hacking back the encroaching vines and clearing the way for me. On weekend mornings he would sometimes buy a big, greasy paper bag of muffins and croissants from the local bakery, then hide it somewhere in the old rural cemetery that stood at one end of our street, placing the bag in the low bend of an oak tree or beneath a marble bench. Then he would lead Jamie and me up to the front gates and point inside. "Go find your breakfast!" he'd say.

He left our mother in charge of all discipline, a role she both excelled at and resented. She was forever creating routines to smooth the terrain of our days. She printed up little menus on quarter sheets of paper, and asked us to select what we wanted for tomorrow's breakfast and brown-bagged lunch. The little checkmarks I made next to *Grape-Nuts* and *Tuna and rice cakes* were contractual agreements, pledges to eat these things because I'd asked for them. She made our lives as predictable as she could, stabilized everything within her reach. Occasionally she would try to turn the tables on my father, and cast him in the role of enforcer.

"Let's all have our teeth brushed and our jammies on before Daddy gets home," she'd say, as he made his slow evening loops around the neighborhood with Tippy. "He won't be happy if you're not ready for bed when he's back."

And sometimes we'd play along. But we knew that he didn't really care what time we went to bed. He was a kind of human prop in her solo campaign to bring order to our lives.

I don't remember when my parents began sleeping in separate bedrooms. One night my father was in the largest room, right at the top of the stairs, and then he was next door in the guest room, where *his* father slept when he visited from England. When I woke up from a bad dream and padded down the hall to crawl into my parents' bed, I found only my mother there, with all the space in the world to curl up beside her. The change held no more meaning for me than that. I didn't connect it with the arguments I often heard through my bedroom floor at night.

My parents never argued upstairs, but they seemed not to realize that the sound of their conflict could travel through the kitchen and up the steps, permeating the space above. Sometimes I would hide on the stairs, or on a couch beneath a blanket, to listen to the rise and fall of their voices. I remember none of their words, only the circular patterns of their debates, the way one subject bled into another, until everything grew muddy with resentment. I never saw Jamie come out of his room to listen to these conversations. He seemed to prefer to shut the voices out, to lose himself in books, or painting, or sleep. He was always the quiet kid.

"Jamie's an IN-tro-vert, and you're an EX-tro-vert," our mother had explained to me once, sounding out the words. "That's why he can't always play when you want him to."

Compared with Jamie, everything about me was frenetic, loud, demanding attention. Visitors to our home were likely to trip over a copy of *Raising Your Spirited Child* lying open on the floor. When those visitors tried to leave our house, they would discover I'd hidden their car keys. Sometimes I'd take a ball of string and tie our guests' legs to the dining room chairs while they sat. I couldn't bear to let anyone walk out the door. I never really trusted them when they said they'd come back.

"You're a changeling," my mother would say to me as I shuddered on the floor after a stormy tantrum. "The fairies swapped my human baby with one of their own when I wasn't looking. You should have gone to some big Italian family where everyone is freer with their feelings. Instead, you got us."

She meant that our family, English on both sides, remained steeped in a generations-old discomfort with volatile emotion. Feelings, especially ugly ones like anger or disappointment, were things to be acknowledged, then mastered. Emotions were the responsibility of the person feeling them, and that person should go to their room for as long as they needed to calm down before coming out. Tears and arguments, it seemed, were things kept for the hours after dark, when everyone else was meant to be asleep.

Some nights, when my parents' voices rose the loudest, I would leave my hiding place and walk out into the middle of their battleground. Standing between them, I would scream, or cry, or knock something over, anything I could think of to draw their attention away from each other and onto myself. It was safer for them to be angry with me, because I, at least, would always be forgiven.

On Sundays, the four of us walked the block and a half to Granny Liz's house for pancakes. The street in between was lined with ginkgo trees, and the smallest breeze would set them aquiver, waving their millions of tiny green fans.

My mother's mother was a tall, wiry woman in her early seventies, with winks of silver in her dark hair, a peace dove tattooed inside her wrist, and a habit of clicking her tongue in the back of her throat. Like my father, she was English, and she still spoke with a clipped accent, even though she was only eighteen when she met and married my American grandfather during the Second World War. Over ten years they'd had four children, my mother the last. My mother once told me she believed that she'd been born to save her parents' marriage, and that she'd failed. They divorced while she was still a toddler, and her father, a politician, went to live in Washington, DC. There on the other side of the country, he remarried and had three more daughters. He and my mother were never close. He died when I was three, and I have no memory of him.

Granny Liz's house had a red front door that no one ever used, and an enormous palm tree, which was being slowly strangled by climbing ivy, growing out front. In her hall closet she kept stacks of pop-up books filled with colorful drawings of dinosaurs, sea creatures, and Galapagos birds that sprang up from the pages when you turned them. Holding one tightly between us, Jamie and I would jostle for the chance to pull the cardstock tabs that made the feet of the blue-footed boobies dance, or spin the wheel that opened the fan lizard's fan.

Granny Liz's pancakes didn't taste like anyone else's because she put nonfat yogurt (she pronounced it "yah-gut") in the batter. She'd cut a knob of butter into the skillet and pour in one spoonful of mixture to test the heat. She'd flip the pancake, then cut it in half to see if it was cooked through. While she poured more batter into the pan, Jamie and I would eat the tester pancake between us, tangy with yogurt and hot with butter.

Granny Liz was an artist, and also taught art at the local junior college. Her second husband, Bill Quandt (Uncle Q's father), had been a photographer who owned a small hi-fi store in town. After his death she married a third time, but in my memory that husband is only gray hair glimpsed over the back of an armchair. By the time I knew her, Granny Liz mostly made etchings, and in her studio she showed Jamie and me how she carved a design into a waxy material, called ground, covering a steel plate. Then she'd dip the plate in acid, which bit into the exposed metal, scoring the design into its surface. Next she covered the plate in ink, and a high-pressure printing press would transfer the image onto paper. Once made, the plate could be used to make print after print.

From an early age, Jamie had a knack for drawing. Unlike me, he seemed to instinctively understand how to set down lines on a page so that a dog looked like a dog, and a house looked like a house. While they sketched, Granny Liz let me touch and hold the many beautiful objects she kept in the tiny cubbyholes of an old typesetting drawer that hung on the studio wall. There were smooth pieces of sea glass and chips of uncut semiprecious stones. There were minuscule milky shells, perfect in their twisting complexity, and tarnished silver keys so small I thought they must open the doors of fairy houses. She kept them only to study and draw, but I felt these were things any museum would be proud to own.

"She's a much better grandmother than she ever was a mom," my mother said wistfully, and more than once. "She never had this kind of time for us." Back then, Granny Liz, a working mother of five, never had enough attention to go around. My mother's childhood had been divided between Granny Liz's modest, bohemian world and her father's affluent, conservative one, and in both places, affection and intimacy were scarce. From Granny Liz, Jamie and I received all the tender attention my mother had not, as though time had both strengthened and softened her love.

The autumn after my fifth birthday party, as the ginkgo leaves along our street turned gold and dropped in silky piles, my mother began spending every available moment at Granny Liz's house. For weeks, whenever I saw her, she always seemed to be halfway in or out of a door, her long hair blowing away from her face, a patterned ceramic bowl of oatmeal in her hand. "On the go," she called it. Our Sunday breakfasts stopped because, she said, Granny wasn't well enough to make the pancakes. Granny had cancer too, she told us, not in her breast or bones, but in her lungs.

Then, one morning in early December, my mother sat Jamie and me down together.

"You know Granny Liz has been very ill."

We nodded.

"Well, this morning I got a call that she was fading, so I rushed over as quickly as I could. Just as I walked in the door she took her last breath, and she died."

She spoke simply and clearly, but her voice broke on the last word. Jamie and I were silent. I must have cried, but I only remember the feeling that she was telling us something very, very important. Granny, like my mother, had had cancer, and she hadn't survived.

Then my mother asked, "Do you want to see her?"

The ginkgo trees were bare as we walked to Granny Liz's house. Their branches crisscrossed the misty sky like something out of one of her prints. The air had the clean smell of earth after rain. I wore a purple wool coat with big purple buttons down the front and held my mother's hand, taking three steps for every one of hers. Jamie and my father walked behind.

We went past Granny Liz's never-used front door, past the tall palm tree with its choke of ivy, and around to the back. In the kitchen, the stove sat cold and silent. The living room looked as it always did, autumnal in the browns and burnt oranges Granny loved. Against one wall stood a statue of an antelope that, any other December, she would already have decorated with beads and tinsel.

As I neared the bedroom door, my steps slowed. Fear gathered inside me. I'd never seen a dead person before. Through the doorway, I saw people bustling back and forth, straightening and arranging. Inching closer, I glimpsed the corner of Granny's bed and, against it, a bit of fabric. I knew the dress, long, colorful, soft to the touch. The familiarity of that dress gave me the courage to move into the room.

At first I kept my vision blurry, afraid to look directly at the figure on the bed. My mother and Antoinette had already dressed her body in the clothes she would wear for cremation. Through half-closed eyes, I saw that they had arranged her two hands over her waist, and I could make out a long rope of silver beads resting on her chest. She was so still. Gathering my resolve, I stepped forward to look into her face. There was something profoundly peaceful in the resting lines of her mouth. She seemed to be smiling.

From my place by the foot of the bed, I watched my mother move toward the silent figure, reach out a hand, and touch the place where her mother's life used to be. The picture bit into my mind like acid, and stayed there, etched.

I would learn later from my aunt and uncles, who had sat by her bedside, that during those final weeks Granny had been trying to strike a bargain with God.

"Take my life," became her prayer. "Take me, and let my daughter live."

My mother was the fourth of Granny Liz's five children. Her brother Bill was ten years older, then came Antoinette, and then Ward. Ward lived two hours south of us, at a retreat and seminar facility called the Mount Madonna Center, founded on the principles of Yoga. Like him, my mother was spiritually curious, and our bookcases held volumes on Buddhism, Jungian psychology, philosophy, and New Ageism.

When I was six, Ward introduced my mother to a couple from Burkina Faso who had come to give a talk at Mount Madonna. Sobonfu and Malidoma Somé were spiritual teachers, speakers, and writers, based in Oakland. They were embarking on a new workshop model inspired by the traditions of the community where they had both grown up as native members of the Dagara tribe. They called the group of people who would come to participate in this year-long program, including my mother, the Village.

For the next year, a group of around fifty people gathered monthly in a large conference room at Merritt College, where the walls were windows that overlooked the hills and the bay. Sometimes my mother made the hour-long trip to Oakland alone. Other times my father would drive all four of us. The first time I entered the conference room, I was greeted by a tall woman with a round, open face, broad cheekbones, and a large gap between her two front teeth. Sobonfu always wore long dresses in colorful prints, with a matching piece of fabric wound around her black braided hair. Her laugh was a kind of joyous scream. She spoke to me the same way she spoke to the adults in the room, as though she saw no difference between us.

The village where she was born, Sobonfu said, placed great emphasis on ritual. There were private rituals and public rituals. Rituals for celebration and for grief. Daily rituals, monthly rituals, and yearly rituals. It was the way people processed the events of their lives, and the way they bore witness to the lives of others. She and Malidoma attributed many of Western society's ills to the loss of rituals in our lives. Without them, they said, people struggled to find meaning. The Village was meant to be a container for ritual, a makeshift community designed to hold shared experience.

For a ritual, Sobonfu said, all you had to do was delineate a sacred space and build a shrine. To make a sacred space, the people involved had to set an intention, agree upon a common purpose. They might define the physical space with a circle of leaves, or stones, or ash. To build a shrine, they needed meaningful objects. These could be photographs, candles, a string of beads, a bowl of water. There were five primary elements, Sobonfu said: water, fire, earth, nature, and mineral. Depending on the ritual, one or more of these elements might be represented by a color or an object. She and Malidoma believed that every person was connected to one primary element, determined by the year of one's birth. My mother was fire, the element of dreams, vision, and strength. Jamie was earth, the element of home, grounded-ness, stability. My father and I were mineral, the element of stories, of memory.

Meetings in the conference room lasted hours, and when Jamie and I grew restless, our father would take us for a hike in the nearby hills. The sky, it seemed, was always overcast on these walks, the wind making the clouds race above our heads.

After the first gathering, I asked my mother if everyone else in the Village had cancer like her, but she said no, they were there for all different reasons. She developed a particular friendship with Jay, a recovering heroin addict who rode a Harley and always smelled like peppermint and smoke. He often spent nights on our couch, and I'd come downstairs in the morning to find his long, slumbering figure poking off the ends of the sofa. At first I felt wary of his huge frame and deep voice, but when he gathered me into his lap, his strong arms made me feel like I was safely strapped into an amusement park ride.

Between the monthly meetings, the members met in smaller groups at one another's homes. When they gathered at our house they always burned sage, and I came to associate the smell with their presence. I was always glad to see Sobonfu, and whenever she noticed me hovering nearby, she would make space for me in their circle. Often I didn't have the patience to linger for more than a few minutes, but she always welcomed me. Children, she said, should never be excluded from ritual. She helped my mother to construct a shrine in front of the fireplace near the kitchen. They set up a long wooden folding table and covered it with a cloth, red for fire. On it they placed photographs of my grandparents and great-grandparents, along with objects representing the five elements. My mother later helped Jamie and me to create similar, smaller shrines for our bedrooms.

Sobonfu told me that these photographs represented my pool of ancestors. I could draw wisdom from these people, she said, even if I'd never met them, because they had joined the great ensemble of spirits. I would stare at the photographs, gazing into each pair of pixelated eyes. I looked longest at the picture of Granny Liz, wishing she could tell me where she was, and what it was like there. *All these people*, I thought, *know what it's like to die.* Over time, these photographs became the closest thing to deities in my spiritual understanding, a kind of ancestral pantheon, the gods and goddesses of my past.

My mother's year with the Village culminated in the most important ritual of all: the rite of initiation. Initiation, Sobonfu explained, had three parts. First, the journey: an uninitiated member of the community must leave the comfort and safety of home and family, venturing out into the unknown. Second, the ordeal: they had to undergo some kind of physical or emotional trial designed to test their mettle, their commitment. Third, the homecoming: they returned to their community and were welcomed home, changed.

"What will my mom have to do?" I asked Sobonfu. I pictured her lifting an enormous boulder on her back.

"Initiation can be different for different people," she said. "Your mother is going through her own initiation. Her illness. Your whole family is going through it."

Because of her illness, my mother did not participate when the other members of the Village buried themselves in the ground up to their necks for hours on end.

Years later, flipping through the black sketchbook, I would come across a photograph of a small pile of objects: tiny shells, ceramic beads, metal keys. They reminded me of the little treasures Granny Liz had kept in the cubbyholes on the wall of her art studio. I pulled out the cardboard chest and searched through the contents until, toward the very bottom, I found a small, unmarked, rattling box. Beneath the photograph in the sketchbook, my mother had written:

My dear friend Jay wore all of these little treasures in a small bag hung around his neck all through the Village initiation ritual. Because I couldn't participate, Jay did everything twice as long—once for him, once for me. This included being

buried in the ground for four hours. These little items were bur-
ied with him.

Some of these items will go to you, some to Jamie, for your
shrines. They carry potent energy and spirit and love. Keep them
hidden and safe. I love you, darling girl.

Your Mommy

I felt a stab of guilt. It had been years since I'd taken down the shrine in my bedroom. I hadn't known how to explain it to the friends who came over to my house. I was in my teens by then, and my memories of Sobonfu and Jay and the Village had begun to fade with time and lack of use. Those gatherings seemed so far away from my present life of geometry tests and crushes and friends that they might have been a dream.

Strangely, the package wasn't labeled, so I couldn't know when my mother had intended for me to open it and find the objects. Turning the tiny mementos over in my fingers I felt a rush of gratitude for the proof they offered that my memories of the Village were true. By then, so much of my life before my mother's death had come to seem like a fairy tale, a long-lost fantasy world of myths and magic. But, I thought, rolling a small bead between my fingers, those years were real, as real as the things in my hand.

I can't remember why we'd decided to move my bed that winter, whether we wanted to see what it looked like over by the window, or needed one of the many things that constantly slipped down between it and the wall—books, socks, plastic swords, magic wands. But when my mother placed her hands under the footboard and lifted, the sound that came from somewhere deep within her body was like a gunshot.

Crack!

There was a fraction of a second, a skipped heartbeat, between the sound and the moment she fell. I was six years old and didn't know what to do, so I stood perfectly still in the doorway. Then she screamed.

I'd never heard anyone make a noise like that before. It sounded like she was being burned. I continued to stand there, paralyzed. I was afraid to touch her, but I couldn't bear the sound she was making, the sight of her writhing on the ground.

Slowly her screams were diluted by breath, until she was able to float a thread of whispered words over them: "Get Daddy." The instruction broke the spell, and I ran. I met my father racing up the stairs and pointed to my bedroom door. He sped past me, the same panic that had turned me rigid sending him into swift, decisive action.

Back in the doorway, I watched as he bent over my mother, touching her body with gentle, searching hands. He spoke in a low, soothing voice, asking questions, making her breathe. Through my terror, I registered the strange, sudden tenderness between them, as intimate as if I'd walked in on them kissing. My mother was always so capable, so formidable. It was hard to imagine her ever needing or receiving gentleness. But now she was crying on the carpet, and my father was stroking her hair. After a few minutes he began to lift her to her feet. It took a long time. Every tiny movement caused her to gasp or whimper. Finally she stood, leaning heavily against my father's shoulder. I stood aside as he supported her, one agonizing inch at a time, across the geometric pattern of my rug and out through my bedroom door.

For weeks after that, my mother seemed in a constant ebb and flow of pain. I don't know whether she saw a doctor, but I believe Dr. Gonzalez's mandate might have disallowed it. She couldn't bear to lie flat, so my father rented an adjustable hospital bed and placed it in the room off the kitchen, so she wouldn't be trapped upstairs alone. During those weeks, I spent my afternoons sitting cross-legged at her feet, enjoying the novelty of a bed in the middle of the house. On the days her pain was tolerable, we would listen to *The Immortal Hank Williams* on cassette, and she would teach me to sew. I learned how to make a pincushion by placing two squares of fabric together and sewing a simple running stitch all around the border, leaving an inch open at the end. Then I turned the work inside out, stuffed it with white polyester filling and a few sprigs of dried lavender, and closed up the gap. On the corner, in an unsteady chain stitch, I'd embroider the initials *G. K.* for my first and last names, and also for my and my mother's first names, Gwenny and Kristina.

Late one night I woke to the sound of sirens, and the blue and red lights of an ambulance dancing across my bedroom walls. I went to my window and saw two paramedics pulling a stretcher from the back. I'd only seen ambulances in movies, and for a moment I thought the stretcher meant my mother was dead. I was too frightened to open the door, so I stayed in my dark room. Footsteps and voices floated up to me from the hall below. I thought I heard Sobonfu's voice, low and anxious. A few minutes, or hours, later I watched through the window as the two men loaded my mother's figure into the ambulance and took her away.

Later I would learn that Sobonfu had been in our house that night, along with other members of the Village, performing rituals to help my mother try to manage the pain. But the pain could not be managed, and finally her agony became so intense that someone called 911. The paramedics, when they came, wanted to lay her flat on the stretcher, but she told them she couldn't stand any pressure on her back, and they struggled to find a way to move her.

At the hospital, scans of her back showed a compression fracture. At some point after the day she fell in my room, lying still in her bed downstairs, her spine had simply snapped. Surgeons worked to stabilize the break with metal rivets, but one vertebra would forever bulge outward, visibly protruding under the skin. The break would eventually heal, but the scans taken at the hospital, her first in years, showed the underlying cause. The cancer had spread to her bones.

My parents told us the news toward the end of spring. By then my mother was sitting up, wearing a bulky back brace over her clothes. After dinner, the four of us gathered in the formal front living room, usually reserved for Christmas or for when my parents gave a dinner party. The living room was painted a deep, velvety red, the two leather couches were red, and there was red woven into the rug on the floor. Usually all the red made the room feel cozy, but that night it seemed violent, like an alarm. My mother and father sat on one sofa, and Jamie and I sat on the other. It was dark outside the big front windows, and on the oak coffee table between us sat a large ceramic bowl of water with four round red floating candles. Four candles, I understood, for the four members of our family. In the careful composition of the moment, I sensed danger.

My mother began to speak. I interrupted.

"Why did the chicken cross the road?"

She stared at me.

"To get to the other side!"

"Okay, Gwenny, it's time to settle down."

But I couldn't settle down. I told another joke. I did silly voices. I got up to sit in my father's lap. I tried every way I knew to stop her from saying the words I sensed were coming. If I did not hear them, they would not, could not be true. Eventually my mother pinned me to the sofa with her eyes.

She said she was dying. She didn't use words like *metastatic* or *terminal*, but she said the cancer had grown and spread, that she wasn't going to get better, and that her doctors were just hoping to give her more time. She said she was still searching for new kinds of medicine, that she hadn't given up, would never give up. She wanted as much time with us as anyone could give her. She wanted to stay with us more than anything in the world. With aggressive treatment, she said, she might have a year.

The word hit my heart like a gong. A year. Twelve months. Fifty-two weeks. Three hundred sixty-five and one-quarter days. Enough time for a grade of school, or to plant bulbs and see them flower. In a year you can grow your hair six inches, learn a new language, heal a broken limb. I'd just turned seven, and until that moment, a year had seemed like a long time. I was shocked to discover that a year was nothing at all. I looked at the four candles on the table between us.

One of them should be burning faster, I thought.

While she was speaking, Jamie stayed perfectly still and silent. He sat wedged into his corner of the red couch, his eyelids drooping as if he might fall asleep. He, I realize now, had his own way of trying not to hear what our mother was telling us. As she went on, his breathing gradually shifted to a shudder; then he began to gasp as tears fell down his freckled cheeks. I'd only ever seen my brother cry when he fell and hurt himself. By the time we all went upstairs to put on our pajamas, we had both sobbed ourselves into exhaustion.

Dr. Gonzalez dropped my mother as a patient when her cancer spread. He said she hadn't followed his regimen precisely enough, and having the scan at the hospital had broken their agreement. He cut ties and left her to figure out what to do next.

I never once heard my mother talk about how she felt when the man she'd trusted turned her away. When I try to put myself in her shoes, I feel such an overwhelming sense of anger and betrayal that it frightens me. I want to stand face-to-face with this person and make him understand that no one in the world could have been more committed than my mother to the task he set her. She was built for this kind of fight. Her demanding, rigorous, uncompromising nature made her perfectly suited to carry out such an exacting program. I believe that's partly why she was drawn to it in the first place, because it allowed her to feel in control. She believed that if she did everything perfectly, held herself to the highest possible standard, she would survive.

My mother may even have believed the failure was her own fault. I imagine her going over the last three years in her mind again and again. Had she missed a pill? An enema? Had she eaten a forbidden bite of meat, or had a glass of wine? A year or two into the program, she'd discovered that the special water filtration system she'd had installed in our house was faulty, and the water she'd been using was just regular tap water, possibly made even less pure by the defective equipment. When she found out, she was furious and heartbroken.

She worried this one mistake might cost her everything. Maybe she continued to blame the years of impure water for what happened. Maybe it was less devastating to blame a machine.

Many years later, I researched Dr. Nicholas Gonzalez and learned that, during the same years he worked with my mother, he was formally reprimanded by the New York state medical board for departing from accepted practices and placed on two years' probation. A few years later, a large-scale clinical study failed to find any proof of efficacy in his treatments. I also spoke to the oncologist who treated my mother directly after Dr. Gonzalez.

"When I met her," Dr. Richardson told me, "here was this bright, young, intelligent woman doing these bizarre things to treat her cancer. The treatments were painful, potentially harmful, and very expensive. I'm not against alternative medicine, and I think that's why she wanted to work with me, because I didn't scoff. I was content to be another cog in her treatment wheel. But some of the things he was having her do were dangerous."

I asked him why he thought my mother, after all her exhaustive research, had chosen the path she did.

"Smart people like her are going to be attracted to this kind of thing. People who don't follow rules, who take risks. They're used to breaking convention. It makes them successful, and also vulnerable."

This made sense to me, but thinking about the consequences of her decision—turning away from conventional treatments in favor of something new and untested—made me dizzy with heartbreak. I wanted to go back in time, come bursting out of a shimmering temporal anomaly like a character from *Star Trek*, and beg my mother to make a different choice. I can't know whether early radiation and chemotherapy would have saved her, but they might have given her a chance. And that was, ultimately, all she was asking for, the chance to fight for her life.

The child psychologist's office didn't look like any doctor's office I'd ever seen before. It had a little kitchen with a refrigerator, a stove, a table, and two chairs on a linoleum floor. Beyond the kitchen lay a carpeted room filled with books, games, toys, and a miniature sand-box sitting on a pair of cinder blocks. The therapist, who told me to call her Judy, was a tall woman in her forties with curly brown hair, a beaky nose, and pleasantly crinkled brown eyes. I looked back at my mother as I passed through the open door. She sat reading in the waiting room, where a white-noise machine steadily whirred. The brace she still wore gave her body an odd boxy appearance under her loose green cotton dress. She'd promised to stay through the entire appointment, but it still took all my courage to let her out of my sight.

During that first session, Judy asked me no questions about my mother or her illness. She watched me play with the little sandbox, digging trenches and tunnels and filling them with plastic figures of animals and Disney princesses. Occasionally she asked about what I was making, and who the people were who populated this little world. I kept my hands busy, and barely looked up at the woman watching me.

"How did it go?" my mother asked as we walked back to the car. A huge weeping willow stood out front, spilling its long tendrils into the street.

I shrugged. I had no words for the solemn feeling inside that room full of toys. I would go back, on and off, for sixteen years.

A few weeks after the first session with Judy, a lady from hospice came to our house and sat with me on the couches in our red living room. I don't know where Jamie was that day, but the lady made it clear she had come specially to see me. She brought out a long roll of fabric, which hung from a thick wooden dowel and was sewn all over with little pockets. On the coffee table between us she laid a dozen little stuffed pillows, like the ones I'd sewn with my mother while she lay in bed. Instead of initials, these pillows were embroidered with words like *sad*, *happy*, *scared*, and *tired*. She asked me to choose all the words that described how I felt when I thought about my mother's illness, and put them into the pockets.

"What about this one?" she asked when I'd finished, pointing to *angry*. I'd left it lying on the table.

I shrugged.

"You know, it's okay to feel angry."

I nodded.

"Maybe just a little bit angry?" she coaxed.

Eager to please, I picked it up.

I wasn't sure why this woman thought I should feel angry that my mother was sick. I couldn't remember a time when she wasn't. It would have been like getting angry about gravity.

I got angry *at* my mother. She wouldn't let me eat all the sugary things I wanted, and none at all after five in the afternoon.

"We'll have to scrape you off the ceiling with a spatula," she'd say when I begged for another cookie.

She frequently lost her temper with me, usually because I wouldn't leave her be when she was on the phone. She'd order me to my room where I'd scream and throw things against the door, fig-uring I'd teach her a lesson by ruining her phone call anyway. Then she'd come charging through my door with a burning look in her eyes. In those moments she seemed so terrifying I'd literally fall to the floor to signal my surrender.

She always took Jamie's side when we fought, because he knew how to be subtle in his provocations, and I had only one mode of response, which was nuclear. It made me especially furious when she imitated my whining.

"I wish you could hear yourself," she'd explode. "I'm going to start carrying around a tape recorder so I can play it back to you!"

But even at my most irate, I knew that we were supposed to have these fights. We had a right to them, and they were precious. Hover-ing behind every argument, every screaming match, were the shad-ows of all the others we'd never get to have. My mother would never tell me what I couldn't wear on a date, would never disapprove of my boyfriend or my choice of college or my job or my parenting. She'd never make passive-aggressive comments about the way I drove my car, or the color I chose to paint a room. I'd never get to ignore her advice about reusable diapers, and she'd never get to ignore mine about politics.

So maybe that was another reason I left that little pillow sitting on the table, because anger was a resource in which I felt poor. I couldn't explain to the kind woman with the soft voice that I wanted so many more years to be angry with my mother. So many more years to sit beside her and stitch our initials into a thousand tiny, useless pincushions.

At the end of spring, Jamie and I joined a hospice-run support group for children of terminally ill parents. We'd arrive together at the low gray building, but were sorted into different rooms according to age. My group was run by two middle-aged women with dark curly hair, and met around a large table in a white room. I hated going, but always felt better afterward. I'd never spent time with other kids whose parents were sick, and it was both strange and comforting to understand that my family wasn't unique, that other people also lived their lives under the constant tick of a clock.

My memories of that white room have a faded, overexposed quality to them. I remember a lot of coloring, with tubs full of nubby crayons. I also remember laughter. The white room wasn't always a sad place. In fact, it was one of the few places where the hard reality of my mother's illness was integrated with humor and play. The ladies who ran the group seemed to understand that sadness in children is not sustainable. It comes in bursts, and then their minds seek out distraction. In that room, it was even acceptable to joke about illness and death. Like generations of girls before me, I had often skipped along sidewalks, leaping from square to square of concrete chanting, "Don't step on a crack or you'll break your mother's back." Among the kids in the support group, I could reveal my secret, guilty punch line: "Oops! Too late!"

There were roughly a dozen of us in the group, but the only faces that come back to me in any detail belonged to a pair of siblings. I remember Carla and José because they left the group only a few weeks after I joined. One afternoon, one of the dark-curly-haired ladies announced:

"Today will be Carla and José's last session."

We all looked at each other, wondering if their father had miraculously gotten better. This, of course, was everyone's secret wish for their parent, but we rarely said it out loud because the point of the group was to accept that it was never going to happen.

"Carla and José will be moving next week to a different group," explained the lady.

Immediately we all dropped our eyes. We knew about this other group, the one for kids whose parents were dead. No one spoke.

"They agreed to come to one last meeting so they could tell us about their experience," she went on, "which I think is wonderfully brave and generous of them."

We stayed silent.

"Well, yesterday," Carla began slowly, "we went to the hospital to say good-bye."

Their father had been on life support for a week, unconscious, his organs slowly shutting down. They explained how they had hugged him, how their mom had cried, how they hoped he'd some-how been able to hear them say they loved him. How they'd left the room before the doctors turned off the machines that were filling his lungs with air and his heart with blood. Neither of them cried as they spoke. To me, they didn't even look sad. They just looked very, very tired. For the rest of the session, we all regarded them with a mixture of pity and awe. They had journeyed to the place we were all headed, and glimpsed the impossible thing on the other side.

After a few months of meetings, the two ladies announced they had a surprise for us. They instructed each of us to write down a secret message to our sick parent on a slip of paper. Then they led us out of the white room and through the glass front doors of the building to the short lawn outside. There a man waited next to a row of venti-lated crates, stacked in twos and full of rustling sounds. We lined up next to the crates and the man took our slips of paper. He opened a mesh door and carefully pulled out a gray pigeon. He explained that these were homing pigeons, trained to carry our messages. When my turn came, he put my paper into a little plastic tube secured around the leg of a pigeon with stripes of white in its wings. Then he handed the bird to me, showing me how to hold it so its wings were gathered under my fingers, and I felt its tiny heartbeat vibrating in my hands. I stepped forward, away from the man and the kids and the other birds, until it was just me and my pigeon. I repeated, in my mind, what I'd written on the scrap of paper, then tossed the little warm, fluttering thing into the air. Both hands, like you might send up a burst of confetti. From nearby, I heard the click of a camera as someone snapped a picture. All these years later, I can look at that picture and see the symbolism of release. I can see that it's meant to be a picture of someone letting go.

But on that scrap of paper, instead of a message, I'd written a wish. It was the same wish I'd wished on every eyelash, every birthday candle, every bridge, tunnel, and dandelion since I'd learned the meaning of superstition. The wish was fourteen words:

I wish my mom would live, and get better, and never have cancer again.

That summer, when her back had healed, my mother put in several raised beds along the back fence, and we tried to grow vegetables. Jamie and I planted rows of carrots, lettuce, and leeks. We made a small trellis of netting against the redwood fence to train runner beans. We walked to King's nursery for bags of rich soil and clear plastic half-pint containers of ladybugs to keep aphids away. King's was home to a large blue parrot who, rather than repeating what you said, would shake his head side to side and screech, "No-o!" when you spoke to him. His wooden perch had a small sign warning curious visitors that he was a biter. I asked to carry the ladybugs on the way home so I could watch their shiny red backs, the tiny black whispers of their legs, the way they bubbled and churned like trapped mercury.

Inside our fence I pulled off the lid and scooped the tiny creatures up in handfuls, spreading them over the property. I placed them on sprouting lettuce leaves, on roses and forget-me-nots, and on the feverfew plant my mother told me was once used to dull pain and cure fevers. When I was four or five, I'd made a game of picking leaves and flowers from our yard and mashing them with a little mortar and pestle I found in the kitchen with the spices. I added drops of water and pinches of soil to form elixirs, which I stored in small colored-glass bottles. Sometimes I'd ask my mother to drink them, hoping they would make her better, and she would pretend to take a sip and then wrinkle her nose to show it tasted terrible. I found this reassuring, since real medicine always tasted bad. As I placed the last crawling, ruby-red handful, I hoped that what I'd heard about ladybugs was true, and that they were lucky.

We began making our own pungent compost under green tarps in a dark corner of the yard. We saved scraps from the kitchen and mixed them with leaves and grass clippings, turning the crumbly mulch with a garden fork to reveal earthworms. In the cool mornings, with our hands in the ground, my mother would talk to us about decomposition, how the death of one plant gives life to another. She told stories about Uncle Q's dad, Poppy Bill, whom she'd loved like a father, and who had died when she was thirteen. She told us how fresh and vivid her memories of him still were. How she could close her eyes and see him take a long pull off his Kent cigarette and blow a row of perfect rings into the air.

The spot we'd chosen for the beds was shaded by tall oaks, and the carrots we pulled up were skinny. The lettuce might have yielded enough for a salad (which I'm sure neither Jamie nor I would have eaten). I think the runner beans did well. I realize now, the vegetables were never the point.

The autumn I started second grade, my mother began climbing into bed with me in the mornings before school. Just emerging from sleep, I'd feel a pair of arms around me, and groggily scoot over to make room in my twin bed. She said she wanted me to remember the way she smelled and the touch of her skin. She wanted to infuse me with some quiet measure of love.

"I'm scared I'll forget you," I confessed to her one day as we lay in bed together, staring up at the ceiling. I felt I was already beginning to forget Granny Liz, dead two years by then. "I wish I had a movie of you talking to me that I could watch whenever I wanted."

That same fall she began her first cycles of chemotherapy. Even compared with her years on the Gonzalez Protocol, the chemo was brutal. Some days she lacked the energy to lift her head. For weeks at a time, each room in our house needed a little pink kidney-bean-shaped emesis bowl discreetly placed at the ready.

"Why are they shaped like that?" I asked Jamie.

"It's so you can hold it up to your chin," he explained. "Also, all the barf can run into the ends so there's room for more in the middle. It's high-tech, if you think about it."

In the waiting room of the oncology ward, I couldn't help but compare her with the other patients, the ones who were thin and bald. *Those people are really sick*, I thought. *Not like my mom.* The hospital smelled of Lysol and bleach, and for a long time I thought disinfectant was the smell of illness. There would be a lot of hospitals after that, and they would all blur together in my mind: the same smells, the same lights, the same winding white halls to nowhere. None of them stuck out in my mind. None seemed like real places.

The week after Thanksgiving, my mother cleared away the many stacks of paper proliferating on the dining room table, and for a day or two the wooden oval emerged like a forgotten face. Then onto its blank surface she placed two small chests, one made of wicker, one of laminated cardboard. Then came the boxes.

There were a lot of boxes: small cardboard rectangles patterned with seashells, and octagonal tins printed with Cicely Mary Barker's illustrations of flower fairies. There were velvet clamshells and tiny enameled containers like the ones we put our lost teeth in. There was a larger wooden box with metal corners, covered in Japanese paper, and a slim cylinder that resembled a slice of a birch branch, until you pulled a hidden tab. There was a box that looked like three turtles stacked on each other, carved from something like bone, and a flat brown leather one that sprang open if you knew where to press. This infestation of boxes made me nervous. I both knew what they meant and I didn't. I'm certain my mother explained it to me, but I was reluctant to let the information sink in. The boxes belonged to a future I wasn't ready to think about.

Sometimes my mother sat at the head of the table, other times along one side, moving as she completed one mysterious task and began another. Some days she'd spend hours sorting objects into the boxes, writing on little white note cards, and threading them with ribbon. The way she'd once pored over the results of clinical trials, she now bent her dark head over bright little packages, tying bow after bow. Tippy would sit with her sometimes, her intelligent black-and-white head cocked, as if a scrap might fall from that table we never seemed to eat on.

Greedy for her attention, I tried to distract her from the project. "Let's go swimming!" or, "Let's play mancala, you can go first."

"Later, honeybun, I'm in the middle of something." The meaning of *later* was narrowing every day.

As the weeks passed, I began to hate the boxes. There were so many of them, like so many years stretching ahead without her. How could the boxes be more important to her than I was? I felt jealous of my future self, the hypothetical girl my mother was thinking about while I was standing right in front of her. I imagined upending the table and sending all the boxes and ribbon and lists and note cards crashing to the floor. But the table was too heavy for me.

That December, my father picked out a seventeen-foot Douglas fir, more than twice the height of our usual Christmas tree. We always cut our own tree from a farm in Sebastopol. When my father wedged one end of the tree into the small wooden trailer hitched to our car and bungee-corded the other end to the roof, it was so long that needle-filled branches covered the top few inches of the windshield.

He placed the tree in our front hallway, where the ceiling went up two stories, and suspended the crown in place with lengths of fishing line. It towered there, nestled in the crook of the staircase. Then he, Jamie, and I positioned ourselves on the steps, tossing bundles of white lights to each other, winding its branches in starry illumination.

Every year in the weeks leading up to the holiday, my mother set Jamie and me to work making gifts for friends and family. In past years we'd done simple things like fold tissue paper into origami stars to hang in windows, or use gold spray paint to turn Styrofoam balls into ornaments. But this year she'd bought dozens of round white candles along with thin slabs of colored wax from which we were meant to cut shapes with X-Acto blades. We would soften the slabs with a flame, then layer them onto the surface of the white globes to create designs. Jamie decorated his candles with dragons and castles. Mine were more abstract. It was an ambitious idea, and we worked each afternoon for over a week, but by Christmas Eve morning we still hadn't finished. Our mother ordered us back to the dining room table, but we'd grown so bored with the project that neither of us could focus. We joked and squabbled. We dripped melted wax onto each other's fingers, and stuck the colored offcuts to our faces.

Suddenly we realized our mother was no longer in the room with us. We wandered upstairs and into her bedroom, where we heard soft sounds coming from the adjoining bathroom. When we stepped inside, we found her sitting, fully clothed, on the tiled shower bench, sobbing.

I'd rarely seen my mother cry. I'd seen her solemn, disappointed, frustrated, and furious, but I don't think I'd ever seen her in despair. Her face was hidden in her hands, but tears worked their way between her fingers. Hearing our footsteps, she bent farther forward, shielding herself. Jamie and I exchanged a guilty look. It hadn't occurred to me that the candles represented something more than party favors, that they formed some crucial part of my mother's vision for this final, perfect Christmas. She looked so defeated, crouched in the dry shower. I tried to say something, but the words wouldn't form in my mouth. Instead, Jamie and I crept silently back downstairs, and got back to work.

I woke first on Christmas morning. I ran down the hall into Jamie's room and jumped on his bed until he agreed to come downstairs with me in search of our stockings. Our father came down next, in his blue terrycloth dressing gown, and put on a CD of the King's College Choir singing Christmas carols. Once her back had sufficiently healed, my mother had gone back to sleeping upstairs, and the rented hospital bed had been returned. Jamie and I gathered our stockings and carried them upstairs to her bedroom.

Jamie and I always made gifts for our parents and each other. That year, my mother had helped me hook a small rug in the design of a red gecko for Jamie's bedroom. For me, Jamie had made a wooden recipe box shaped like a log cabin with a little painted window and door, a thatched roof, and a brick chimney. The roof lifted off to reveal a stack of index cards, and the chimney had a little slot to hold one at a time. My mother had already filled in several cards with family recipes: Granny Liz's pancakes, the flourless chocolate cake we always had on our birthdays, the gluten-free chocolate chip cookies she'd invented because Jamie couldn't eat wheat.

After all the gifts had been opened, my father took me on a long walk around the neighborhood with Tippy. We strolled the length of our street, passing the entrance to the cemetery, its gates open, its tombstones deep in shadow. Mist still covered the morning, turning things dewy and gray. We greeted some family friends sitting on their front porch with a tiny puppy, a Christmas present for their children. The puppy, an Australian shepherd, wobbled on his oversized paws, lifting his nose to the vast, unexplored world.

When we got back to the house, Jamie and my mother were still in bed together, and I could tell he'd been crying.

My whole life I'd felt secret things pass between my mother and brother. They'd always seemed to belong to each other in some way I didn't. They even looked alike, with their dark hair, straight noses, and hazel eyes. I was fair like my father, and both our noses bent slightly to the right, though he always said that his was the result of an old rugby injury. I felt like the changeling, the fairy baby swapped at birth, the one meant to observe and learn to belong in this human family. Sometimes I wondered why a fairy would ever want to belong to a human family when it was the hardest, most painful thing in the world.

In spring, I sat with my mother on the wide redwood porch behind our house, while the hairdresser's clippers buzzed like an angry insect. Her hand squeezed mine as the long straight hair fell to the ground in clumps. As the blades did their work, her bare skull glimmering through the remaining hair made me think of a pirate, and I stifled the urge to rudely say, "Ahoy!" Or maybe I did say it. I always seemed to say the wrong thing at the wrong time. We left the hair on the deck for the birds to weave into their nests, but she saved one long braid, about the thickness of a licorice whip, and gave it to me. I put it in a little metal box on a shelf in my room. For years afterward, I'd open that box to breathe in the fading scent of her shampoo.

The chemo worked.

At the end of the year my mother's doctors had allotted, new scans showed her condition had stabilized.

I absorbed the news with a feeling of stunned anticlimax. After a year of thinking we were celebrating our last Fourth of July together, our last Halloween, Thanksgiving, Christmas, the very last of my parents' elaborately executed birthday parties, we were instead back at the beginning, looking forward to another year of lasts. Another year, the doctors had said, no more than that.

It was the best news we could have hoped for, and yet . . .

A year.

A year would not even make a dent in the time I wanted with my mother. I wanted time to waste, time to forget that our life together had any end at all.

We found we couldn't sustain the urgency with which we'd been living our lives. It was exhausting, spending every moment together, living every day to the fullest.

That same year, Mrs. Wiggles Rocket Juice ran into trouble. A rash of *E. coli* poisonings in California had been traced to another company with a similar product. This led to new state laws around the sale of food and beverages. Mrs. Wiggles was a small business and couldn't afford to comply with the new standards. My parents were forced to consider selling the company, then to consider that the company might go under. My mother still oversaw business and marketing strategies from home, but left the daily operations to my father. Their worry over the business seemed to merge with their worry over my mother's illness until the two things were indistinguishable to me, a murky cloud of adult concern.

My parents had never spoken to Jamie or me about money. There had always been enough. The cost of my mother's treatments had never threatened to bankrupt our family. We'd never had to choose between her medical care and other necessities. When both my parents worked they could afford childcare, and when managing my mother's illness became her full-time job, a wonderful woman called Elisabeth came three days a week to cook, clean, and do the laundry. The threat to the company marked the first time I had any inkling my parents were concerned over finances, and it would be many years before I understood how serious that concern had been.

One afternoon, at the peak of the crisis, my mother walked out to my father's office, a small building behind the house, and found him holding a shotgun. When she asked what he was doing, he confessed he'd been thinking of ending his life.

I can only imagine my mother's feelings, watching her physically healthy husband cradle death in his arms. *No,* I imagine her thinking, *you can't die. You are the one who has to live.*

What she actually said, I'm told, was that he had promised to take Jamie on a bike ride that afternoon. Didn't he remember that? It seems that this was enough to convince my father to put down the gun and go on living. Afterward she quietly removed both the shotgun and my father's hunting rifle from the house. When I finally heard this story, long after the company had successfully sold, it sounded like something that had happened to another man, in another family. How could the person holding the shotgun be the same person who threw the magical birthday parties, who made up scavenger hunts and dressed up in ridiculous costumes and sang to me at night? The person with the gun, I felt, had nothing to do with me at all.

In third grade I changed schools, moving from a private K–8 to a public elementary school in our neighborhood. Jamie had skipped a grade, and was already at the public middle school. It didn't occur to me that this might have anything to do with our parents' financial problems. My mother said she wanted us to make friends in our neighborhood.

I liked my new school because I could walk. I found it easier to leave home on my own feet. I hated to watch either of my parents drive away from me.

At first I was only allowed to walk to Proctor Terrace Elementary with an older girl who lived on our corner, one-half of a pair of twins. In the fifth grade, my mother promised, I could walk alone. Proctor Terrace was the same school my mother had attended, more than thirty years earlier, and my morning route was the same one she had taken.

My best friend at my new school was Becca. She was tall, with straight, silky brown hair and a face full of freckles. When the invitation came to spend the night at Becca's house, I was so excited that I forgot I'd never spent an entire night at a friend's house before. My father drove me over on a Saturday afternoon. We played in her backyard with a kitten she had just adopted, a Siamese called Alexander. She showed me how to make Lipton iced tea, and how to flavor it with mint pulled from a patch by her back door. Later we played with her mother's makeup, painting dark lines over our eyebrows, spreading purple eyeshadow on our cheeks. We used nothing the way it was intended, because we didn't mean to make ourselves beautiful, only to make each other laugh.

The weight began to gather in my chest when the sun went down. I sat through dinner with Becca's family, pushing the unfamiliar food around my plate. At home, my father would have cooked me scrambled eggs, or plain pasta with butter. It was a family joke, the way I only ate beige food. I would have eaten at the kitchen counter with my father and brother. My mother would be sitting at the dining room table reading and writing, or she'd be up in her room.

After dinner we played in Becca's room with her Barbie dolls. I was not allowed Barbies at home (my mother said they didn't present a positive female body image) so, of course, I adored them. When it was bedtime, I settled in my lavender sleeping bag on the floor next to Becca's bed, and her mother came in to kiss us good night.

In the dark, the feeling in my chest began to spread toward my throat. My father would be walking Tippy now, her red leash slung around the back of his neck as she trotted in front of him into the dark. My mother and Jamie would be in their rooms, each reading in the glow of a lamp. The room between theirs, my room, would be empty.

The taste in my mouth was like metal. My cheeks tingled and my hands grew hot. I could hear my heart, and I began to worry that Becca could hear it too. *Go to sleep!* I commanded myself. If I could only fall asleep it would be morning, and it would all be over. My breath came faster, and I shoved my pillow into my mouth.

"I won't die while you're gone," my mother had promised me years before, when I'd been frightened to leave her side for even a second. "That's not how cancer works. It won't be sudden. We'll have a long time to get ready."

I believed her, and still this animal was trying to claw its way out of my chest. Becca's mom was still awake when I went out into the living room. She called my father immediately when I asked, and he was there in minutes.

At lunch on Monday, Becca told all the girls at our wooden picnic table that I had left her house in the middle of the night.

"She wanted her daddy," Becca said, and they laughed.

My ears burned. I understood her words were meant to shame me, though they were simply the truth.

My mother's hair grew back in little fluffy curls, completely unlike the hair she'd lost. She looked strange to me in curls; they softened her face, diffusing the lines of her cheekbones and the sharp point of her chin. She pulled her new hair back with large purple snap clips to keep it out of her eyes.

Every afternoon when I walked in the door from the third grade, she would call out, from wherever in the house she happened to be, "Gwenny, Gwenny! You're home!" Greeting me, as Davey used to, with total, uncomplicated joy. Then she would tell me to go practice the piano.

We had an old upright wooden Yamaha, and five days a week I was meant to sit on the lacquered wooden bench and play my exercises for thirty minutes. My teacher came on Thursdays and would immediately open the black composition notebook where she wrote down my assignments, to check the upper left corner of the page where I kept a practice tally. There were rarely more than three lines there, but it never occurred to me to falsify the record, and add a few more.

My mother had also taken piano lessons as a child, but hadn't stuck with it. "I only *wish* someone had made me practice when I was your age," she said.

In her mind, this daily practice would prepare me to become a certain kind of person, one who could accompany Christmas carols, delight a room with show tunes, or gently underscore a party.

Someone who could sit down, anywhere in the world, at the same set of black-and-white keys and make music.

But the hours I was meant to practice each week were investments in the future, and the future was a place I had learned long ago to fear, to resist. I did not want to become a person who played the piano, I wanted to remain a person with a mother.

After a few years of piano lessons, Jamie chose to learn the bagpipes. *He* practiced diligently, generating a steady stream of noise that suggested a procession of cats and geese being methodically strangled in the room over the garage. I listened, over weeks and months, as the discordant racket slowly resolved into something bearable, and finally into something beautiful. He'd had seven years with our mother before she got sick. Somewhere in that time, he must have learned what I hadn't: that the future was coming, whether you prepared for it or not.

My mother survived the second year her doctors had forecast, and was given another.

She still read to us in the evenings: *Dealing with Dragons*, *Wise Child*, *Five Children and It*. As we listened, and squirmed, and whacked each other with pillows, my father would lean back against the bed's wooden footboard, slicing apples and handing out the cool, sweet slices. My favorite book, the year I turned nine, was *The Golden Compass* by Philip Pullman. It was about a girl called Lyra who was a little older and much braver than I. My favorite thing about the story was that Lyra had grown up believing her parents were dead, and then discovered, at age eleven, that they were alive. I was devastated when my mother read the last sentence and closed the book.

Jamie was allowed to read the next book in the series, *The Subtle Knife*, but my mother wouldn't let me. She said it was too frightening.

"I'll read it to you when you're older," she said, "when you're ten."

Just as eight was the right age to walk to school with a chaper-one, and thirteen was the right age to pierce my ears, ten was the right age to read the frightening book.

But that fall, when I was still nine, her vision began to fail. She needed my help to thread an embroidery needle. She bought a pair of lit magnifying glasses that made her look like she was about to perform surgery. Another set of scans showed the cancer had spread to her brain.

The procedure to treat the brain tumor required screwing a metal halo to her skull to keep her head still. Holes were drilled just above the outer edges of her eyebrows, where the bone was thickest. The doctors successfully beat back the tumor, but the damage to her sight remained. By winter, the hospital bed reappeared, this time in her room upstairs.

After she came home from the hospital, someone sent her a sing-ing Valentine. Two boys in tuxedos and two girls in velvet bodices, silk skirts, and pearls came from the choir at the local high school. They stood in our kitchen and sang, and my mother stopped what she was doing behind the counter and listened. She smiled at them as they ran through their repertoire, clapped when they were finished, and offered them a warm drink, before they headed back out into the chilly air. After they left, she sagged a little.

"Poor things," she muttered. "I must have looked so frightening to them."

She touched the round Band-Aids covering the holes in her tem-ples, each soaked through with a splash of blood.

"Like I had horns," she whispered.

I stared at her. The changes to her appearance had happened so gradually, I'd barely noticed them. I tried to see her through a stranger's eyes. Her face and body were swollen from steroid treat-ments, and she leaned on a walker. Her fluffy chemo curls fell to her shoulders, and through them the twin blood-soaked bandages peeked out.

The timeline of my mother's illness grew more and more uncertain. I began to think of her as an outlier, an exception, existing on the fringes of known science. I continued to believe, secretly, that she would survive forever, no matter how many times everyone told me that it was impossible. Sometime soon, they said, she would begin to actively die.

I made a grim kind of game out of giving my mother survival goals. "Live until our birthday," I'd say, sitting on the foot of her bed while she tried to write a card or stitch a seam. Then "until the end of school," "until Christmas." For long periods the decline in her health would be slow, almost imperceptible; then suddenly she'd lose the ability to walk down stairs, or understand the rules of a new game. I wanted concrete markers, stretches of time I could count on, knowing she wouldn't disappear. "Live until the new millennium," I requested, in the early days of 1999. Each time she'd smile and say, "I'll do my best."

Three days after the singing Valentine, I turned ten. That morning my mother woke me early with a small box made of shiny black cardboard and printed with colorful birds. Threaded on the curly pink ribbon was a white note card that wished me a happy birthday. Inside the box, resting in cotton wool, was a little oval amethyst brooch backed with gold. Beneath *Happy Birthday*, the card read: *pg. 16.* I looked up at her.

She handed me a spiral-bound ten-by-twelve-inch sketchbook. It was black, with a picture of two red pears on the cover. I turned to page 16, where I found a photograph of the same brooch I held in my hand.

I felt a strange sense of unreality, of two things overlapping that were never meant to touch. This was the first of the little packages my mother had prepared at the dining room table. I was sitting next to her, reading the words she'd intended to be read after her death. This was the future. We'd crossed some threshold, and caught up with the later versions of ourselves we'd been chasing. I was now the ten-year-old she'd imagined when she'd wrapped up the amethyst brooch and pasted its picture in the book, and she was both the voice in the book and the flesh-and-blood woman beside me. And still, neither of us knew what would happen next. I left the brooch at home when I went to school; I couldn't imagine wearing it to the fourth grade.

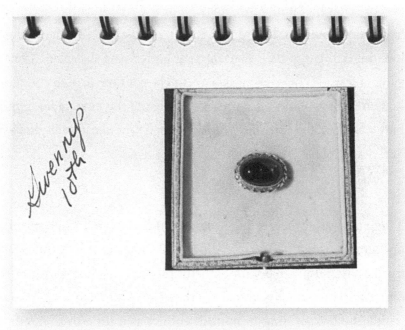

This amethyst brooch was given to me by Granny Liz for Christmas or my birthday one year. It had matching earrings w/ screw-backs. I asked G. Liz to have them converted for pierced ears. She took them back to have it done, and then lost track of them and we never laid eyes on them again. xox Mommy

That afternoon my mother took me to pierce my ears, three years early. At the local mall, I picked out a pair of tiny white crystals. I sat in the large reclining seat while two sales assistants, each with a little plastic gun, stood behind me. My mother sat in front and held my hand. We all counted to three.

I looked in the lighted mirror while she paid for the crystal ear-rings, and for a pair of little gold hearts I could wear once my ears healed. I noticed one earring looked higher than the other.

"No," my mother said, squinting hard at me, "they're the same."

The sales assistants reminded me to turn the posts every day, and to clean my ears with rubbing alcohol.

Out in the parking lot my father, who'd waited for us, opened the doors to the car. About to get in, my mother suddenly stopped. She took my face in her hands and tilted it one way, then the other in the wintry sunlight. "You're right," she said finally, "they're crooked."

We went back to have the left ear done again. I asked what I should do about the first empty puncture.

"It'll go away on its own," one of the ladies said. "The holes close up fast when there's nothing there to keep them open."

In the following months, my mother became more and more self-conscious about her appearance. Sometimes she'd turn it into a joke. Jamie was now a teenager, tall and lanky, and navigating a new social landscape. One morning at breakfast he made some surly comment about our parents embarrassing him, and she slowly pivoted on her walker to face him.

"I," she said slowly and dangerously, "am going to put on my bag-giest, rattiest clothes, mess up my eyebrows"—she suited the action to the words until her brows looked like startled caterpillars—"black out my front teeth, and show up at your school to tell everyone that I am Jamie's mother!"

I collapsed in giggles.

"Sometimes, Jamie," she said, "talking to you is like a day with-out sunshine."

But soon after, she asked me if I would prefer it if she didn't come to my basketball games anymore. It took me a moment to understand what she meant.

"It won't hurt my feelings," she said.

I told her I wanted her to keep coming.

One afternoon my mother's cousin Sandy came to take her for a spa day. She had a massage and a skin treatment, and then she had her makeup done and her hair blown out straight. She came home looking disappointed.

"I don't know what I expected," she said. "I guess I thought I would look like me again."

Her blown-out hair was shiny but limp, and emphasized how round her face had become from all the steroids pumped into her system. She looked swollen and stretched.

The summer after her cancer spread, my mother had set Jamie and me to work making scrapbooks to record our childhoods. Going through the stacks of old photographs, Jamie and I had pulled out snapshots of our mother as a teenager, or in her twenties, before we were born.

"Mommy, you were so pretty!"

She'd hold the picture for a moment.

"Yes," she'd say. "I wish I'd known."

Passing by my mother's door one day when I was ten, I heard the soft murmur of voices coming from inside. The door was partly open, and through it I saw my mother standing naked in the center of the room. Beside her, Sobonfu held a glass jar full of something that looked like wet coffee grounds. As I watched, Sobonfu dipped her fingers into the dark liquid, then lifted them to my mother's body, slowly tracing designs onto the skin of her chest, her shoulders, her back. I hadn't seen my mother's naked form since I was young enough to bathe with her. I could see the place where her fractured vertebra still bulged beneath the skin, the shiny pink lines of her surgical scars. The care with which Sobonfu touched her was so different from the clinical precision I'd witnessed in her doctors' gloved hands. It was the kind of tenderness I'd only ever seen given to children.

As I leaned closer, the bedroom door creaked loudly and both women turned to look at me. I took a step backward, and waited for their faces to tell me what this meant, whether I should feel ashamed of having seen it. For a moment, a wordless consultation seemed to pass between them. Then Sobonfu smiled, and my mother held out her arms to me. I stepped inside the room, and Sobonfu handed me the jar in her hands. From the smell, I could tell it was full of ashes. They had been mixed with water, and were the consistency of thin paint. I dipped my fingers into the jar, and together Sobonfu and I traced the ashes over my mother's flesh.

I didn't ask what the ritual meant. Everything I'd observed about Sobonfu over the years told me that our touch was intended to heal, to bring balance to what had become chaotic. I tried to focus all my energy into my fingertips, wishing I could reach through her skin and pluck out what didn't belong. My mother closed her eyes, as if to better absorb our touch. I painted dots and lines, mimicking Sobonfu's patterns, and then making my own. Sobonfu made no suggestions, no corrections. She said there was no way to do it wrong.

The summer after fourth grade, my father announced he was taking Jamie and me to England to visit his family. I was excited, because I hadn't seen my British cousins in years. My mother showed me how to pack my suitcase, an old-fashioned brown one with a combination lock and a little leather strap. She rolled up my socks and underwear and stuffed them into my shoes to help them keep their shape. She laid my dresses, unfolded, in the bottom of the bag, packed everything else inside, and then turned the edges of the dresses over the top, so they wouldn't crease. I had a special red leather case for my passport. My father reminded me that, while we were in the UK, I should ask for the "loo" or "toilet" instead of "restroom." The night before we left, he made me practice curtsying in the mirror, in case we ran into the queen.

My mother was exercising in the pool as we packed the car to leave for the airport. She treaded water in her purple one-piece, supported by a long foam noodle, her curly hair clipped up on top of her head. A woman from a caregiving agency sat by the edge of the water. The woman would stay in the house with her while we were gone.

"Good-bye, sweetie," my mother called cheerfully from the water.

I stood by the concrete steps in my gray Gap sweatshirt, a backpack over one shoulder full of snacks for the plane. Until that moment, I hadn't felt the gravity of leaving her behind.

I thought of her getting out of the pool after we'd left, leaning heavily on the metal railing, and walking into an empty house. I thought of her eating dinner with the caregiver in the kitchen, or up in her bedroom. I thought of her waking up in the morning, the day stretching out in front of her. Suddenly I couldn't imagine how we'd all decided it was all right to leave her. She smiled up at me from the blue water. Guilt poured into me like sand, making my feet heavy. I wanted to wade out toward her, into the middle of all that blue, but the car was packed, and Jamie and my father were waiting.

I lingered by the pool's edge, hoping she would ask the questions that would allow me to tell her how awful I felt. But she just floated and smiled and waved good-bye.

All through the ride to the airport I felt tears gathering, and once we were past the security checkpoints they poured out. At a café, I cried myself sick. I told my father I didn't want to go to England anymore. It was too late, he explained, I'd feel better once I was on the plane. My father gave me his cell phone to call home.

"I love you," I sobbed into the black Motorola.

"I love you too, honeybun," my mother said brightly. "You'll have so much fun!"

The flight from SFO to London Gatwick was ten hours. I cried, and slept, and cried some more.

We spent about two weeks in the UK. I visited my grandfather and played with my cousins and went to the Tower of London and fed the birds at St. Paul's Cathedral, but I swore to myself that once I was home, I would never abandon my mother like that again.

The wheelchair made our world smaller. Boundaries and obstacles, once invisible, materialized everywhere. We rented a van with a hydraulic lift to lever her in and out. At first I wanted to push her everywhere, but I was bad at navigating corners and often banged her toes into walls. Jamie was better. He was careful and conscientious, and stronger. He would wheel her smoothly down a hallway, bending his head near hers to talk.

She had to spend more time in bed, which was hard on her body. The constant pressure of blankets on her toes caused her nails to become ingrown, so we got a little metal cage to place over her feet underneath the covers. Her body had to be turned regularly to prevent bedsores. She kept photographs of her younger half-sisters' new babies taped to the bed's metal handrail, to look at while she lay on one side for hours.

Caregivers came daily to sit with her, to help her from bed to chair and back again, and to give her medicine. A family friend owned the caregiving agency, and I got a job there after school, filing papers and filling out forms on a little electric typewriter to earn extra pocket money. I loved the noise the typewriter made; every keystroke sounded important. Sometimes I answered the phone. The callers might have been surprised to hear a ten-year-old on the other end, but I clearly spoke the name of the agency, and asked how I could help. I'd had plenty of practice. It drove my mother nuts when parents allowed their children to answer the phone and waste callers' time. I always answered our home phone by saying crisply, "Hello, this is Gwenny Kingston. May I ask who's calling please?" Often the caller would ask to speak to "Ms. Mallard." My mother's last name was Mailliard (pronounced "my-yard"), and her rule was that if they couldn't pronounce her name, they didn't get to speak to her.

Each time my mother's doctors predicted the end was near, a wave of friends and relatives would descend on our house, everyone hoping to get in one more conversation, or hug, or memory. I loved it when our house was full of people, even though I knew why they were there. I loved slipping in and out of the little pockets of adult conversation. Jamie usually retreated into his room, but I wandered. Each knot of people welcomed me. Hands were placed on my shoulders or head, arms gathered me into laps. Everywhere I went, I felt loved, wanted. It was as though the house itself, which I loved like a person, had come to life, voices pouring from its walls, bodies blooming among the furniture. I wished they would stay forever, and I would never have to be alone again.

Each day when I came home from school, there would be at least five or six people gathered in chairs around my mother's bed, walking up and down the stairs to fetch tea, books, and ice chips. I sat on the staircase where everyone would pass me and stop to ask about my day, to comb their fingers through my hair. I wanted contact with all of them, but I stayed away from my mother's bedroom while they gathered, because inside that room everyone was crying. From my place on the stairs, I saw them leave with swollen eyes. One day I watched one of my mother's younger half-sisters, visiting from across the country, come rushing out the bedroom door, in her black overalls and white socks, and bury her face in her hands, her dark hair falling forward.

After she left, I went to my mother's room and slipped into bed with her. We lay next to each other and talked about school and my friends and the books I was reading. Staring up at the ceiling, I noticed a few daddy longlegs spiders gathered in the corners.

"Ew! I'll get the DustBuster."

"It's all right," she said, "I've named them. That one's George and that's Alan."

I looked up at them. One had a fruit fly suspended in its invisible web and was poking at it with its spindly legs. For just a moment, I had a tiny inkling of how bored my mother must be. Her eyesight wouldn't let her read or sew. She got books on tape from the library, and sometimes passed them on to me. I always loved being read to.

She missed being outside, and when the weather was good, she would ask someone to open the French doors that led from her room out onto a small wooden balcony facing the backyard, and let sounds and smells pour in on the breeze. Occasionally a bright-green katydid would find its way through the swinging screens, and she considered this very lucky. She adored their stillness, and the way their folded wings looked like a new leaf. Whenever I found one, I would catch it gently in my hands and bring it over to her. A bit of freshness from outside. Then I'd take it onto the balcony and hold out my flat palm, waiting for it to leap.

On the morning of my eleventh birthday, I rolled out of bed and went straight to my mother's bedroom. She was already awake. A small wrapped box sat, along with the black sketchbook, on the little retractable wooden tray of her hospital bed. We wished each other happy birthday. She was forty-eight.

Inside the box was a small rectangular pin of blue and white enamel that showed a watery horizon broken by waves, a little sailboat, and a windmill.

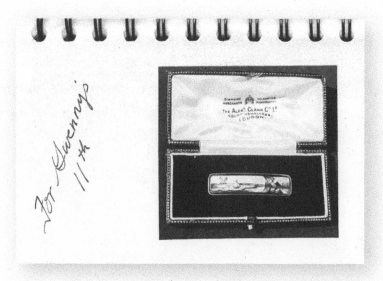

I don't know why I was so smitten with this pin. I saw it at an antique show at the Fairgrounds. I thought the blue and white would suit you and I liked that it seemed to tell a story.

Like the amethyst pin the year before, I thought it beautiful, but struggled to imagine wearing it. Girls my age wore thin necklaces, stud earrings, and occasionally a woven friendship bracelet around their wrists, but they didn't wear any real or valuable jewelry, and no one wore brooches. I imagined pinning this pretty thing onto my gray cotton sweatshirt, and heading out to the playground for recess. In fifth grade I was developing my tetherball game. I could hold the court through five or six opponents before defeat, when I'd immediately take my place again at the end of the line. I pictured the smooth yellow ball hurtling toward me and shattering the sailboat and the windmill, the pin falling onto the blacktop, trampled beneath someone's Skechers.

Running my fingers over the smooth enamel, I said, "Maybe we could make a plan to think of each other every year on our birthday, wherever we are."

"What time?" she asked.

I looked at the clock. "Eight a.m.?"

"It's a date."

By fall, my mother withdrew into sleep for longer and longer periods. She no longer called out her greeting when I came home from school, and when I came into her room to sit by her bed and talk, she often seemed groggy and confused. After a while, I would only poke my head in to say hello before going to my room to do homework, or call my friends. One evening, sitting on the back deck in the last of the twilight, my father asked me if there was anything I wanted to tell her, while she could still hear me.

"If there's anything you haven't said, now might be a good time."

I thought about it for a moment. "I want her to know that I'm sorry for the times she wanted us to do something together, and I said no because I was doing something else. I feel guilty about that."

"I think that would be a good thing to say. She probably has regrets like that too. You could talk about that."

Later that night, I went into her room.

"Hi, sweetie," she said thickly, from beneath the film of sleep.

"Mommy," I began, "do you ever feel guilty about the things we didn't get to do together?"

"N-no," she said, struggling to focus on my face. Her jaw was slack, and her tongue seemed thick and rubbery in her mouth. "No, because I kn-know I"—she took a deep breath, gathering enough air to push out the next words—"did the best I could." She closed her eyes again. I looked down at her, her big loose T-shirt, the tubes taped to her arms. I could smell the residue from the wipes used to clean her up after she used the bedpan. I felt I'd gotten the interaction all wrong. I wanted her to wake up and ask me the right questions. I would have told her that I knew she'd done the best she could, the best anyone could. I would have told her that I felt guilty every day about the hours I spent away from her, about the times I *wanted* to be away from her and the horrible, stupefying sadness that filled the room where she was slowly losing herself. I would have told her I felt guiltiest of all that part of me wanted this to finally be over, so I could begin to remember her the way she used to be, instead of the way she was now. But her eyes stayed closed.

The year before, as promised, my mother had let me read *The Subtle Knife*, and I'd finally discovered what she'd found so frightening about the book. In the sequel to *The Golden Compass*, Lyra journeys into another world overrun by creatures called Specters. The Specters feed on human consciousness, draining their victims of all interest and curiosity, of the very will to live. But they cannot harm children, only adults. In one scene a man and his young son are fording a river, trying to flee a band of Specters, but the creatures overtake them. They eat the man's soul, leaving his body standing in the river. His son begins to struggle in the deep water. He calls out to his father for help, but the man simply stands there, watching his son drown, indifferent, unreachable. This was her fear.

That fall, *The Amber Spyglass*, the final book in the trilogy, hit shelves. It was a five-hundred-page brick, twice the length of the previous books, but Jamie and I devoured it in days. Then my mother asked Jamie to read the book aloud to her, so she too could learn what happened next in the story.

For the next few days, Jamie came home after school and sat by her bed and read to her. He didn't perform all the different character voices, the way she had, but he offered up each word clearly in his newly deepened voice, pouring the story into her ears. He read to her about Lyra's adventures in other worlds, about witches, and scientists, and armored bears. Sometimes I would stop and listen for a few paragraphs, but in that room I felt something passing between my mother and her firstborn, a relationship predating my existence, an older claim. He made it about halfway through the book before she asked him to stop. She said she couldn't follow the story anymore. It made her anxious to lose the thread, to have to ask him to go back over things again and again. She seemed to be moving into a place where words could not follow.

It was a Wednesday, so I had a therapy appointment with Judy in the afternoon. At nearly twelve years old, I felt I'd outgrown the playroom, so we met in the little office next door where she spoke to parents. Judy sat in an armchair, and I sat on the couch. My mother had been asleep for several days, an oxygen cannula under her nose.

"Will she wake up again?" I wondered out loud.

"I don't know. This is what happens toward the end, they sleep more and more."

I nodded; the ladies from hospice had said the same thing. I felt strangely numb, my emotional energy drained by all the waiting. For so many years I'd been afraid that my mother would die suddenly while I was at school, or spending the night with a friend, or away on a trip. I felt I'd spent my entire life at home, watching her. But I'd never imagined death could be like this, so slow, so boring.

It was raining as my father drove me home. We were alone in the car because Jamie had quit therapy years before, but I'd come to like the routine of it, the couch, the quiet. Sometimes we only talked about friends or homework, but I liked knowing that I could tell Judy anything.

Once we got home, I went upstairs to check on my mother. She looked the same as she had the day before, and the day before that. Antoinette, Sobonfu, and Sandy were gathered around her bed. Uncle Ward was away in India where he spent a few months each year, and we'd called to tell him that she seemed to be nearing the end. He'd booked a ticket to come back early, but was still traveling. Someone had held the phone to my mother's ear as he spoke to her from thousands of miles away. "I'm coming," he'd said, "but if you can't wait for me, it's okay." After saying hello to all the visitors, I went downstairs to find Jamie, who was playing games on his computer.

Our mother had asked us, years before, whether we wanted to be in the room when she died. "It's completely up to you. You decide what you want, and we'll try to make that happen. And you can change your mind, even at the very last second."

Jamie and I didn't discuss our mother's illness with each other. We couldn't seem to find the language. We only talked about it with grown-ups who could help guide the conversation, teaching us to name our feelings. But separately we had each told our mother that, yes, we wanted to be in the room when she died.

But that night Jamie and I were both downstairs, staring at the computer screen. I'd always imagined that, when it finally happened, I would know. I'd sense something, a door in my mind would open, or close, or there would be a change in the light. But I noticed nothing. Jamie kept playing his game, and I kept murmuring encouragement, until our father came downstairs to find us and tell us that this part of our lives was over. Later that night, after seeing my mother's body, Jamie gathered up all his computer games and threw them out the back door into the rain.

My mother had asked to be cremated, and the clear plastic bag containing her ashes came along with a separate bag full of hardware, which a technician had pulled from her remains with a magnet: long screws and steel rivets that had held her damaged body together.

She'd hoped her ashes could be buried in the old part of the rural cemetery at the end of our street. But that section, with its wonderful gnarled trees and dappled light, had long since stopped assigning new plots. She talked with us about other places we might scatter her remains—the Pacific Ocean, her family's ranch in Mendocino County where redwoods grew, our own back garden—but nothing seemed right. Then my mother's oncologist, Dr. Richardson, heard that she was looking for a spot in the cemetery. His family had a plot there, with an open space reserved for him. He gave it to her.

The headstone my father ordered was made of rose granite, a simple prism with rounded edges. Jamie designed a Celtic knot for the top of the stone. The front showed only her name and the dates of her life. The back of the stone read: *Mother of Jamie and Gwenny*.

Ten years later, I would run into Dr. Richardson at a memorial service, and thank him for giving my mother her place in the cemetery. I would tell him what it had meant to me to be able to visit her there over the years.

"Did I ever tell you," he asked, "how your mother asked me for the plot?"

"No," I said.

"Well"—he straightened his bow tie—"she said that she wanted to be buried in that cemetery because as a little girl she used to play there, and she remembered peeing behind the headstones." He burst into laughter, his shoulders shaking, his eyes moist. "How could I say no to that?"

It was still raining the day of the memorial, and the event stays smudged in my memory, as if left out in the weather. My father is missing from the day completely, as if he wasn't there. My mother had been so surrounded by people over the last several years that my father had been pushed to the background, and after her death, those same people rushed to surround me. The memorial was held on a property near Calistoga often rented out for weddings and retreats. I wore a blue velvet dress, and I had a cough. When we arrived, Sobonfu, wearing a yellow rain slicker, was leading construction of a natural archway of willow branches and fresh flowers outside the entrance of a large tent.

My cough made it difficult to keep quiet while people spoke. I remember one of my mother's doctors taking the podium and comparing her to Captain Kirk from the original *Star Trek* series.

"I felt like an officer under her command. It was my job to explore and bring back new technologies."

He spoke of her willingness to take risks, to try new therapies, and to tolerate pain and discomfort.

"When I had something promising, I'd call her up and say, 'Kristina, I have dilithium crystals for you!' and she'd say, 'Beam me up, Scotty!'"

I remember none of the other speeches, but at the end Jamie stood up to play the bagpipes. He walked to the front of the room and arranged the bag on his hip, but instead of putting the chanter in his mouth, he moved to the podium and approached the microphone. No one had expected words from us, certainly not from him, the introvert. He spoke not because it was expected, but because he wanted to. His voice was steady, and I felt the room collectively lean in.

"I just wanted to say—that all the people here today—are really a testament to the person that she was."

I looked up at him, my brother, nearly sixteen, and so tall. I felt suddenly, enormously proud of him. He kept it brief, just a few sentences, but people drank them in. The room brimmed with gratitude, as though he had just answered some unspoken question about whether we would be okay. Then he lifted the dark wooden reed to his lips, filled the bag with breath, and played the first notes of "Amazing Grace."

Every day after school, in the months after my mother's death, I would walk in the back door, make a snack, and head upstairs to her bedroom. Behind the white door, the room had reverted to the past. Everything looked just as it had in the years before she was confined to a hospital bed. The carved oak bed frame was back in its place. The room was sunny and peaceful. It still smelled like her, as if she'd just stepped out a moment before.

Sitting on the bed or in the beige recliner, I'd balance my snack on my knees and watch television on the white twelve-inch set that sat on one of the low bookcases beneath the windows. My mother had only ever let me watch PBS, but my father didn't care. I often watched TV in her bedroom all afternoon, and later I'd stay there to do my homework, spreading my books out on her floor.

Wednesdays at 10 p.m., I flipped the channel to UPN to watch the next episode of *Voyager*. I anticipated the series finale with a mixture of excitement and dread. I didn't want the show to end, but I did want to see the crew get home. In the final installment, which aired at the end of May, Captain Janeway found a way to get her ship back to Earth by traveling back in time.

For months afterward, I dreamed that Captain Janeway was my mother, or rather, that my mother was Captain Janeway: still out there, somewhere in the universe, traveling in an alternate timeline. Though if my mother had ever discovered time travel, I felt certain, her destination would have been the future.

PART TWO

It was a hot day in July. I was twelve, and my mother had been dead five months. All afternoon a cold pain had built somewhere near my center. It reminded me of the feeling when my father used to reach into my open mouth and yank out a loose tooth. I didn't tell my father about this new pain. Instead, I closed the door to my room and went to the cardboard chest.

In the months since my birthday, the chest had sat in the corner of the window seat, where I could see it each morning from my bed. Its presence both soothed and frustrated me. After the bright, brief excitement of unwrapping the amethyst ring and reading my mother's words, the hard realization that I would have to wait an entire year for her next message began to sink in. I'd never been good at waiting. In the wake of her death, a year seemed, once again, like a long time. So I was thrilled to have a reason to open the domed cardboard lid again so soon, even if the pain in my abdomen was growing, becoming a twisting, grinding throb.

The letter marked *Gwenny's First Period* came in an envelope fastened with a cardboard button and a length of golden thread. The envelope bulged in the middle, and when I shook its contents onto my rug, a gray audiocassette in a clear plastic case clattered out along with the letter.

When I was very little and couldn't fall asleep, my mother would slip a tape into the player beside my bed and let the voice read me to sleep. Over the years, the shelves in my bedroom had filled with dozens of glossy cases holding recorded children's books, fantasy series, and mystery novels. Nearly every night of my life, I'd drifted off listening to a voice reading a story; the most comforting thing in the world.

I fed the cassette into the tape deck and pressed Play. After a few seconds of silence, my mother's voice emanated from the speaker. I looked down at the letter and followed along, the smooth pages crinkling in my hands, as she read to me.

Dearest Gwenny,

Your first period! How I wanted to share this with you. I wanted to share in your pride and excitement about this wonderful change from girlhood to young womanhood.

My first period arrived when I was eleven years old and I was in the 6th grade at Proctor Terrace School. (I wonder how and when yours has begun.)

I was a little worried and afraid, and excited, and not at all sure about what to do. I wasn't absolutely certain my period had actually begun; what if something was wrong with me? (None of my friends had ever mentioned their period starting, yet.) But, I had a feeling I had just stepped across a divide and was changed forever.

When I got home from school that day, I showed my underpants to Granny Liz. She said something like, "Oh, the Curse. You wait here while I go to the store. I'll be right back." She came back with sanitary napkins and a sanitary belt. Then she said something like, "You know what these are for." She handed over the stuff and that was my first step into young womanhood.

I so much wanted to give you a different perspective because to me starting your period means the possibility of bringing your

*own Gwenny or Jamie into the world. What joy!! This is the be-
ginning of your life in the community of women. If only I could be
here with you and tell you how proud I am of you and how much I
cherish your growing femininity and deepening sense of yourself.*

At the words "sanitary napkins," I paused the tape and went to
my closet. Parting the curtain of hanging clothes, I reached into the
very back and pulled out a thick package of maxi pads.

"So you'll be prepared," my mother had said, years before, as
she slipped them onto a shelf. She'd even thought of that.

I squeezed the white and purple packaging. They were the kind
with wings.

*I had counted on being here with you to be your ally in this
rather amazing and complicated experience called growing up.
Here you are facing this important change without me.*

*Losing your mother so young might make you doubt yourself,
your right to happiness and love, to life and a future. Please let
go of any such doubts. You have the right to have the best possible
life that you can make for yourself.*

*My greatest hope is that having known you were so loved as
a child that you will be able to choose for your friends and com-
panions people who love you for your own true self. That you will
know how to give yourself a happier, kinder, more supportive and
loving life than I knew how to give myself. Because I grew up
with parents who did not know how to express their love for me,
never having been given love themselves when they were children,
I didn't know how to give myself a loving, nurturing life as a
grown-up. I pray that though I didn't get to stay with you nearly
long enough that somehow I have been able to help you feel so
loved and valued in the time we had together that you will know*

that you are worthy to be loved and nurtured as an adult and that
you, in turn, will be able to freely express your love and caring
for others.

I've chosen this ring for you to celebrate your "menarche" or
first period. To me it represents the innocence of your maidenhood
and the flowering of your womanhood.

A bow of pink silk ribbon, threaded through two holes in the
corner of one page, held a delicate gold ring set with seed pearls in
the shape of a flower, with a chip of turquoise at their center.

I found with the start of my period the beginnings of romantic
feelings. The Beatles had just arrived from England on their first
U.S. tour. I transferred most of my romantic yearnings onto them
during the sixth grade. Because girls tend to mature physically
more quickly than boys do, I found the boys my own age shrimpy
and young and hardly worthy objects of romance.

But something begins to happen at this age where wanting the
attention of boys often causes girls to change their behavior and
forget their own aspirations. Girls worry that if they are smart or
competitive or athletic they will be threatening to boys and less
likely to win a boy's favor. Gwenny, you have a first-rate mind.
Please try to remember that any boy who needs you to be less than
you are to like you and feel comfortable with you is not a boy who
is worthy of your affections. You might look to a much older boy
for a special relationship. I did. But then you must grow up too
quickly to be able to meet the expectations of the older boy.

I guess what I'm trying to say is that you just need to hold
tight to yourself for the next few years. You will be hard-pressed
to find a boy your own age who is mature enough to handle all
that you are capable of being and doing and an older boy will

cause you to enter his world rather than your learning to make a world of your own that is appropriate for you.

You have such a passionate nature, little Gwenny. If you can, try to save your passion for yourself; for your own interests, your love of learning. Don't be too quick to squander your passion on pleasing another's notion of how you ought to be in order to be attractive to him. Girls are so quick to give themselves away in their longing to belong to someone. You belong to yourself first and foremost.

I know it can seem like growing up takes forever but, in truth, birth to adulthood is only about one-quarter of your life. Three-quarters is spent looking back at youth. Enjoy it while you have it and enjoy each bit of it to the full. Take time to make friends with yourself. Take time to learn what interests you, what your opinions and feelings are, find your own sense of the world and which values you hold most dear. We must become ourselves, become a human being. It's a process. It isn't automatic and it isn't guaranteed. We must find ourselves anew at each stage of life.

Please try not to lose yourself. These are challenging years. Try to be true to yourself and your quest for finding your purpose in this life. Call on me for help when you feel confused. Call on Granny Liz. You carry our love and wisdom in your heart and you will find something of us if you look there.

I love you my darling one,

Your Mommy

I lay on my back, the tape player resting on my sore belly, whirring with static. Tears trickled from the corners of my eyes and pooled in my ears. My mind was full. I'd never given a thought to my mother's romantic life before she met my father. She and I had grown up in the same neighborhood, gone to the same school, yet (until her death) I'd never pictured her as a little girl, never considered the manner in which her childhood had unfolded, just down the street, all those years before. For the first time, but not the last, I regretted my lack of curiosity about my mother, about the person she had been for most of her life, in the decades before I was born. Somehow she had known that I would one day want to know these things about her, and she had answered questions I hadn't even thought to ask.

Staring up at the blank expanse of my ceiling, I thought about September, when I would start at Santa Rosa Middle School, and for a moment I imagined my mother starting there too: just another girl in my class, another stranger in her own changing body. The pearl ring twinkled on its page, round and bright as a coin. I rewound the cassette to the beginning, and pressed Play.

Full speed ahead, and damn the torpedoes!" my father shouted as we careened through the streets in his white Toyota. My father, never cautious behind the wheel, pushed the needle of his speedometer to new heights the year I turned thirteen. Without my mother's careful planning, our family of three ran perpetually behind schedule. My father, Jamie, and I would leave our house at 7:58, bound for two different schools that each started at 8 a.m. That year, the city installed three new stop signs along the route my father drove each morning. The neighbors had complained.

Every so often a police car pulled us over on that stretch of road. The blue-uniformed officer would approach my father's window and tap twice on the glass.

"Do you know the speed limit on this street?"

"Erm, twenty-five, isn't it?"

"Correct. And do you know how fast you were going?"

"How fast?"

"Fifty."

"Ah." My father would look slightly sheepish. "Right, fair enough." And he'd stretch out his hand for the ticket. Occasionally they let him off with a warning. His English accent usually went over well with law enforcement.

When Jamie got his license, he began driving our mother's old Volvo station wagon with the vanity plate that read HLY MKRL for "holy mackerel," his favorite phrase when he was small. He drove fast like our father, and when I got my license a few years later, I would drive that way too. All three of us drove like we were being chased, as though, after so many years of living urgently, we didn't know how to slow down.

Santa Rosa Middle School, where my father dropped me each morning, was made of gray concrete and sealed behind a tall chain-link fence. It looked like it had been built to cage more than to educate, as if the transformation of its students from children to teenagers was something to be contained. My favorite part of the campus was the long cement breezeway that housed rows of metal lockers. Mornings and afternoons, the corridor echoed with the sounds of hundreds of students lifting latches, slamming doors, spinning the dials of combination locks. I papered the inside of my locker with cut-up photographs and notes written in milky gel pen. I loved it the way a child loves anything that can be fastened and kept private. Those few cubic feet of real estate, mine for two years, offered the narrowest bit of purchase on this new, alien terrain. During my first week, I kept looking up and down the rows of little metal doors, wondering which locker had belonged to my mother. If I squinted my eyes, I thought I could almost glimpse her among the mass of bodies: tall like me, but with dark hair cut into heavy bangs, a plaid skirt, tall white socks, a girl I'd seen only in black-and-white photographs at the bottom of a shoebox.

Sometimes I'd imagine this girl walking beside me through crowded hallways on my way to class. Other times she'd appear in the back of a classroom, saying nothing, scratching away with a pencil at a desk until the lesson ended. I'd catch a glimpse of a checked skirt disappearing through the door to the girls' bathroom, and tell myself it was her. The frequency of these impressions waxed and waned; after all, she was only an echo, a thirty-year-old reverberation of a girl who had once walked those same halls. After school, she and I took the same route home. We both avoided the busy main road and wound our way through side streets. We both turned left onto McDonald Avenue. Then she would peel off into the white house with the red front door, while I continued down the street alone.

On the morning of my thirteenth birthday, I pulled a small pouch from the chest. It was made of blue silk and held closed by a single metal snap. I opened the black sketchbook to the page indicated on its white tag.

> *I bought these plain pearl stud earrings when I was living back east. I think I got them before I started work on Capitol Hill to try to look more like a grown-up. Or, I may have gotten them for job interviews after graduating from business school. What I do remember was they were my first purchase from Bloomingdale's department store, an absolute institution on the East Coast.*
>
> *Love, Mommy*

I held the twin milky spheres in my palm. They were beautiful and serious. Thirteen was the age my mother had originally promised I could pierce my ears, the age, in some traditions, when a girl becomes a woman.

My mother had never spoken to me about her time in Washington, DC, but I knew, through the strange osmosis of childhood, that she had left California in her mid-twenties to work as a legislative aide to a senator. I pictured my mother, young and long-limbed, in that postcard city of domed marble and carved stone, rushing up and down its many flights of steps, the business of the nation on her mind. It would have been the 1970s, and I imagined her in skirts and blazers, the pearl studs gleaming in her ears. What was she like then?

This woman at the height of her energies, unencumbered by husband or children, everything around her teeming with urgent life.

I took the earrings off again before leaving my room that morning, and placed them on my dresser. I didn't feel nearly sophisticated enough to wear them. There may have been times and places where thirteen-year-olds were considered women, but though I'd grown to nearly my full height, I still felt every inch a girl. Several years later I would wear them in a high school play, and lose one forever in the darkness backstage.

About a month after my birthday, Antoinette came to stay with me while my father went out for the evening. We'd ordered takeout and were just emerging from the parking garage outside the restaurant when Antoinette stopped abruptly beside me, her eyes fixed on something beyond the passing cars.

"What?" I asked.

I followed her gaze, and glimpsed them through the plate glass window of our favorite Thai place. My father and the woman were brightly lit, as though on display in a shop window. The woman had red hair. As I watched, she got up and walked toward the back of the restaurant, where the restrooms were located. Antoinette paused on the sidewalk for another moment before stepping forward.

"Come on," she said.

We walked through the swinging glass door and approached the takeout counter. My father, seeing us, stood up from his table. Antoinette walked over to him and said something low and apologetic that I couldn't hear. I stared at the back of the restaurant, waiting for the woman to reappear. When she did, Antoinette tried to hurry us out with our food, but my father introduced us calmly, as if he'd always meant for us to meet this way.

"Gwenny, this is Shirlee," and we shook hands.

In the year since my mother had died, my father had dated several women. There had been someone called Helen, who met my father and me at a diner called Mac's on Thursdays. I had ordered grilled cheese sandwiches and ice cream sundaes and made awkward conversation. Jamie, by virtue of age and gender, was mostly allowed to stay home.

I asked my father a lot of questions about Helen. I wanted to know how they met, and what he liked about her. I wanted to know whether she had any children, or wanted any.

"Do you love her?" I asked one day in the car, as we sped through the streets toward Trader Joe's.

"No," he said after a long pause, and my whole body relaxed in the passenger seat.

"Just as long as you're not having sex," I said.

My father said nothing and gazed straight ahead as we zoomed along. The day he told me he'd broken up with Helen, relief flooded through me. Some strange, indefinable danger had passed.

The first thing I registered about Shirlee was that I knew her. She was the mother of a boy I'd gone to school with since the third grade. David and I had never taken much notice of each other. He hung out near the basketball courts, playing pickup games during lunch. I felt a sliver of panic expand behind my chest as I held her red-nailed hand in mine and said, "Hi."

Safely in the car with our dinner, Antoinette let out a long breath.

"I considered just turning around and leaving the food, but I thought he might have already seen us through the window."

"I know her," I said, feeling as if a small elevator inside me was plummeting. Her familiarity made everything more real. This was not someone who would easily vanish from my life like Helen, a suddenly empty seat across the table at Mac's. Antoinette and I drove home in silence, each of us separately lost in thought.

Over the following months, I grew accustomed to the sight of Shirlee's floral overnight bag at the foot of the stairs, signaling that the empty space in my father's bed would be occupied that night. I don't think my father knew that, at thirteen, I still sometimes crawled in next to him when I couldn't fall asleep. My inability to sleep away from home had resolved after my mother's death, but I often woke in the middle of the night, breathless from nightmares. On these nights, I'd wander down the hall from my own room and curl up on top of the blankets near my father's knees to listen to his slow, rhythmic breathing. He slept deeply, and I always returned to my own bed before morning, soothed by the presence of another warm, familiar human.

Shirlee seemed to stay at our house whenever David was with his father.

"I don't like it when she spends the night," I said once.

"Well"—my father spread his hands—"it's not your decision to make."

We argued for a few minutes, then:

"Just to be clear: Is this our house? Or is this your house, and I just live here?"

He thought for a moment. "This is my house," he said slowly, "and you live here."

I felt a tiny shift in the ground beneath my feet.

"It must feel like your mother is being displaced. Like you are being displaced," said Judy, as I sat on the couch in her office the Wednesday after the argument.

"Why does he have to date *her*?" I asked. "Why a mom from my school?"

"That must feel embarrassing," she said.

"I think they're having sex," I said.

"Probably," she said.

I did nothing to hide my anger about my father bringing this new person into my life. I was cold and distant without being technically rude. That is my memory, though I would not care to see a videotape of my behavior. I learned to walk a tightrope of words, choosing the ones that revealed my anger but could not land me in trouble. I had always loved words, but never wanted to weaponize them till now. My sharp tongue made me feel temporarily powerful, in a situation over which I had no real power at all. I feared that any warmth I gave her, any lowering of my defenses, would signal to my father that his actions were not causing me pain. It was an exhausting protest, but I mounted it anyway, holding fast to my resentment as though it could save me from drowning in simple sadness.

I had the luxury of disliking my father's girlfriend because I had a wealth of wonderful women already in my life. I'd inherited my mother's circle of friends the way another daughter might receive a fabulous collection of designer gowns. These were the women who had spent countless nights on folding cots in hospital rooms, driven hundreds of miles to doctors' appointments, and flown across the country to consult specialists. They were married and single, mothers of four and childless. They were lawyers, business owners, and homemakers. For the first few years after my mother's death, they invited me to an annual luncheon on the anniversary, and we swapped memories over soup and vegetable platters. They could describe a much more complex person than the mother I remembered. They spoke of a woman whose sharp tongue and intellect could impress, but also wound.

"Boy, sometimes the things that would come out of her mouth," Sandy said, shaking her head, "I'd just have to go in the other room and cry."

I shifted guiltily in my chair, thinking about the pleasure I was learning to take in making my own words sting.

"And she didn't mean for it to hurt," Sandy went on, as though defending my mother from herself, "her brain just worked so fast, and she didn't always think about how her words would affect people."

"She gave wonderful advice," a woman called Anne said. "Because she had to be in bed so much, you always knew where you could find her. I think she liked the distraction of thinking about someone else's problems."

"But then," another friend chimed in, "you'd have to deal with the follow-up. If you said you were going to make a change in your life, quit a job, break up with someone, the next time you saw her she'd ask you what you'd done about it, and if the answer was nothing she'd make you feel about two inches tall. The problem was, she was always right. That's what made it so frustrating, and why you always kept coming back."

I tried to square these anecdotes with the person who had read me stories and tucked me in at night. She was also the person who had fought so bitterly with my father, the person who for years had acted as CEO of the juice company. I knew her in the context of my family, but her friends knew her as a woman who predated marriage and children. Some had known her since she was my age.

The luncheons eventually petered out, but many of the women who attended remained in my life. Over the coming decades they would listen to my romantic problems, take me shopping, and help me move. They would lend me money, buy me furniture, and take my calls in the middle of the night. They would each mother me differently, according to their strengths.

That spring, everything about Jamie signaled that he was on his way out the door. He was seventeen, and acceptance letters were arriving weekly from colleges with fancy, faraway-sounding names. For him, this new version of our family, morphed from square to triangle, was temporary, a holding chamber leading outward to the rest of his life. Come fall, he too would leave an empty room behind.

He graduated from high school on a blazing June afternoon that turned into a frigid June night as the principal worked his way through all five hundred names in the senior class. I picked out Jamie's black-clad figure easily on the football field, because he was doing a kind of faux-dignified walk, his hands clasped behind his back, his head bent, like some aged civil servant. I tracked his tiny form to its seat as the last notes of "Pomp and Circumstance" (or, as Jamie called it, "Pompous and Circumstantial") flowed out of the speakers. I cheered along with my father and my mother's siblings from our perch in the bleachers when Jamie's name was called.

Weeks later, I sat on the floor of his bedroom while he packed to leave. He'd decided to defer from college for a year and enroll in a travel program called Leap Now. Jamie had skipped the sixth grade, and disliked being perpetually younger than all his classmates. This way he would begin college at eighteen, like the other freshmen.

The black backpack he would carry on his travels through Ecuador, Peru, and India was larger and covered in more straps than any backpack I'd ever seen. When he fastened the belt around his narrow hips and tugged on the buckles to tighten it around his chest, it looked more like armor than luggage. On the carpet beside me sat Jamie's wicker chest, the twin of mine. Jamie would turn eighteen in April, on another continent, four thousand miles from the chest, and from me.

"Maybe just take this one," I suggested, pointing to the package marked *18th Birthday*. But Jamie shook his head. He didn't want to worry about it getting lost or stolen.

"What about this?" I held out his old teddy bear. Its fur was matted and its head had once fallen off because he spent so much time hitting me with it. Afterward I'd clumsily sewn it back on for him. I wanted him to take something to prove that his leaving home would cost him some tiny fraction of what it was costing me. Again, he shook his head. I waited until he was in the bathroom, then shoved the teddy bear into the very bottom of the backpack. He'd find it weeks later, wedged among his wool socks.

That night my father and I drove Jamie to the International Departures area of SFO. I hugged him good-bye, and he kissed my forehead, a thing he'd never done before: a benediction. I tried to hold back the tears until his tall figure had turned away and stepped through the sliding glass doors to the terminal. I didn't want to make him feel guilty, but I already missed him the way you'd miss sunlight or wind, something you never thought you'd have to learn to live without.

Fourteenth birthday:

After Poppy Bill died, Granny Liz, Uncle Q & I went to England to visit with G. Liz's mother and sisters. They gave me this sweet little leaf pin. I was fourteen.

Years before she died, my mother had told me that my father would one day remarry, and that it would be all right. My mother's family tree was heavily grafted, divorces and premature deaths leading to second and third marriages, some bearing fruit and creating even more confusion about how we were all related. Granny Liz had been married three times. My grandfather married twice. All my life, Thanksgiving dinners had been full of stepparents and half siblings and half-siblings-in-law. I knew that not all stepparents were like the ones in fairy stories, that they didn't all lock their stepchildren up in basements or send them into the woods to be eaten by wild animals.

"She might be someone really wonderful," my mother had said, "like Poppy Bill."

She asked me to keep an open mind, and I promised her I would try.

It was the last day of classes before my ninth-grade winter break, and my father surprised me by picking me up after school. Usually I walked home in the afternoons, a leisurely contrast to the rush and scramble of the morning drive to class.

"It's raining," my father said by way of explanation. "Come on."

He pulled out onto the street, but instead of pointing the Toyota in the direction of our house, he began to wind through the side streets.

"Where are we going?" I asked.

"I thought we'd pop in and say hello to the Qs."

My aunt and uncle lived near the center of town in a house they'd painted a bold shade of orange, something between tangerine and pumpkin. My father pulled up in front, slightly blocking the driveway with one bumper. We wouldn't be staying long.

Aunt Carole answered the door when he pressed the bell, and I could tell by her face she hadn't known we were coming. My father had sprung this on both of us. He put his hand on the small of my back and guided me into their living room, as Uncle Q emerged from the kitchen. We all sat down on the green sofa and matching chairs.

"Gwenny," my father said, "I have something to tell you."

It had been years since I'd sat through one of our family meetings, bracing myself for news I did not want to hear. At fourteen, I was too old to tell knock-knock jokes or wedge my way into someone's lap. Besides, this was not our house, and I was a guest. I wondered, looking at my father's anxious, hopeful face, if that was exactly the point in being here.

"Yesterday," he said, wasting no time, "I asked Shirlee to marry me."

Though I sensed they were coming, his words hit me like a fist. My jaw buzzed with adrenaline, and I tasted its metallic bitterness in my mouth. I could feel everyone's eyes on me and I tried to control my expression, but tears leaked from my eyes and puddled in my lap.

I could tell my aunt and uncle were surprised as well. I wondered what Uncle Q thought about this. He was my mother's brother, and now her husband was going to marry someone else. But my father had always been close with the Qs and they had welcomed Shirlee when he introduced her as his girlfriend. Uncle Q's own father had been my mother's beloved stepparent. I looked away from them, my face hot with embarrassment. I loved them both, but I hated being observed while I felt so vulnerable.

Instead, I looked at my father, his red-gold hair, his California tan, his nose that bent the same way as mine. For most of my life, he and I had been allies, but now something had changed. I had become an obstacle to what he wanted, and he had overcome me. There was no defense to mount; the battle was already lost.

"Congratulations," I whispered, forcing the single word past the burning lump in my throat. He looked so relieved, so happy, I almost felt sorry for him. How frightened he must have been of my reaction to have staged it all this way.

"Thank you," he said, smiling at my aunt and uncle. They looked back at him, then at me. He was beaming. I was shaking, and soaked in tears. They both congratulated him, but my aunt held me in her arms for an unusually long time on the doorstep before we left.

Keep an open mind, my mother had said. Why did I find that so difficult? I didn't like the way Shirlee always waited for my father to open doors for her, or how she laid her red-nailed fingers on his arm. I didn't like that she made us sit down to dinner "as a family" when my family had generally eaten our meals scattered across three or four different rooms. I didn't like that a thoughtless comment from me could send her into a storm of tears, and that my father would then be sent to make me apologize. I didn't like performing the displays of affection she seemed to expect from me. I didn't like that she wasn't my mother, but there was nothing she could do about that.

At home, Shirlee was waiting with champagne and sparkling cider. I said congratulations to her as well, and watched as she filled the tall flutes. David must have been with his father that night. Jamie had finished his gap year and was back for the holidays after his first semester of college. As far as I could tell, he didn't seem to miss home at all. When he walked into the room I could see that he already knew about the engagement. My father must have told him separately. Again, I wondered what intuition, or strategy, had caused him to divide us.

After the toast, Jamie and I excused ourselves to go to the video store and rent a movie. We got into our mother's old Volvo and fastened our seat belts. Jamie pulled away from the curb and sped down the road that ran beside the cemetery where she was buried. It was the road that led to the video store, the road that led to most places. I noticed that Jamie kept turning his head to look at me.

"What?" I asked.

"Nothing," he said, "it's mean."

"Go for it," I said.

"Well"—he grinned at me sympathetically; he would be leaving to go back to college in Pennsylvania after New Year's—"it sucks to be you."

Two days before Christmas, my father, Jamie, and I drove to the farm in Sebastopol to cut down our tree. By now the enormous Douglas fir in the front hallway had become tradition. We always got our tree late, but this year we'd waited for Jamie to arrive home from college. It would have been too strange to go without him. Shirlee did not accompany us, preferring to stay in the warm house listening to Ella Fitzgerald sing Christmas carols. David would be with his dad until Christmas Day, and I was grateful for an hour or two alone with my father and brother. As we approached the entrance to the farm, we were greeted by a small sign with a picture of Santa Claus saying CLOSED.

"Oops," I said, already trying to picture a treeless Christmas.

But my father pulled up hard on the parking brake and got out of the car. He went around to the trunk and pulled out the handsaw he had brought, then walked toward the closed gate and hoisted himself nimbly over the wooden rails.

"Come along," he called back to us.

Jamie and I followed him over the fence, and past another large sign that said NO TRESPASSING. Our father had brought a stiff yellow measuring tape, which he fed up the trunk of one tree after another, looking for seventeen feet exactly. The winning tree had a bare patch on one side, which my father said would be perfect to place against the stairs. He and Jamie took turns sawing through the thick trunk, shedding layers of clothes, growing warm with the effort. We carried the huge tree back to the gate on our shoulders, my father in front, Jamie in the middle, and me at the back, bearing the tiny weight of the crown. We wrestled it over the fence, covering our hands and faces in sticky, pungent sap. My father lashed our tree to the roof of the car, its waving, unnetted limbs reminding me of a lazy, compliant animal. Before we left, he placed the price of the tree in cash in an envelope, and slid it under the door of the little building where they served cookies and hot apple cider. Back in the car, triumphant, we tore away from the farm as though the police might come at any moment. Streaking along the winding roads, past vineyards and dairy farms, away from the scene of another of my father's minor heists, I felt hopeful. Some things, it seemed, would stay the same.

During the too-brief weeks of Jamie's school vacation, he and I stayed up late, knocking on each other's bedroom doors at night to look through old photo albums and swap well-worn stories, our father's impending marriage tipping us into a nostalgic binge. A few days before Jamie had to leave for the airport, he and I went to the red fireproof safe in my father's office and pulled out a stack of black VHS tapes that had been sitting there for most of a decade, untouched.

I'm not sure how we knew where to find the videos, or even that they existed. But the information was there in both our minds. We both knew our mother had hired a videographer to record them when she first learned her cancer had become terminal, nearly five years before her death. During those years, the videos had fallen from our thoughts, blotted out by gratitude that she continued to survive. The fact of them remained hidden in our minds, until our fresh hunger for the past dragged it from the darkness.

We took the tapes into our mother's old bedroom, fed the first clattering cassette into the VCR, and settled ourselves, me on the bed, Jamie in the recliner.

"Ready?" I asked. I couldn't name the feeling nudging at my insides as I looked over at him.

"I guess so," he said, and I jabbed the remote.

After a few frames of static, a plinking piano melody filled the room, and the screen showed a still of the impatiens that grew in our backyard superimposed with the words *Reflections of a Lifetime.* Jamie and I rolled our eyes. It struck us both as embarrassingly sentimental. We were teenagers, after all, and believed ourselves sophisticated.

And then she was there.

As the music faded, a woman appeared sitting against the low redwood fence in our backyard, a cluster of oak trees behind her. She wore a blue cotton button-down. Her long hair was pulled back in a low ponytail, the dark wisps of her bangs blowing in a light wind. Pearl studs glimmered in her ears. It was nothing like looking at a photograph; it was like being in the room with her.

Hello, Jamie, said our mother. *Hello, Gwenny. My little duckies. I love you so much.*

Oh, it seems strange, making a video for you, and it probably seems a little strange watching this. But it's a way for me to leave something of myself. Actually, the idea for this came from little Gwens. Do you remember, sweetie, when you and I had our very first heart-to-heart chat about the possibility that I might die while you were still just little? I asked you if there was anything you could think of that might help, and right away you said, "You know, Mommy, I wish you could make a video where you say, 'Hi, Gwenny!' and I could watch it whenever I needed to be with you." So I thought that was such a wise and good idea, that here I am!

So I'm making this now, this is the first of October 1996, beginning of fall, and I thought it would be a really good idea to do this for you while I still look like me, and I look good and healthy and the way I would like you to remember me. But I don't want you to think I'm doing it because I've given up all hope, or because I've stopped fighting to be here with you. And actually someone's standing behind the camera, holding a picture of you, the one that's the magnet on the refrigerator that Daddy and you made on Mother's Day for me. So I feel like I'm really talking right to you, and it's helping a lot.

I was already crying. I realized that the nameless feeling was fear. I had been afraid of what might be on these tapes, afraid to revisit the heartbreak of those years when I had heard, over and over, that there was no hope, and that my mother was doomed. I looked at Jamie, and saw his eyes begin to fill as well. I wondered if we'd made a mistake. I couldn't have explained why the image of my mother, speaking bravely, even cheerfully, about the battle lying ahead of her filled me with such a desperate sadness. The emotions coming through the screen were too big, too complicated, and somehow too adult. I worried that, if I tried to absorb them, they might drown me. The trouble was that I had asked for this video when I was seven, but now I was twice that age. I now understood what would've been invisible to me then: that keeping her voice light and controlled was costing the woman on the screen just about everything she had.

I want, first of all, to talk to you about what I'm trying to do to be ready, and to help you be ready. I've spent the last several months writing you letters. I'm still writing them.

And the way the idea came to me was I was thinking of the story of Vasilisa, where the mom is dying and she gives her daughter a little doll that she keeps in her pocket. And then when times are difficult and she's faced with some big challenges that she's really still too little and inexperienced to deal with, she takes her doll from her pocket and the doll gives her the clues that she needs to know which path to take. And what that doll represents is her own intuition, and her own inner wisdom, and her mom's love for her. And I realized how desperately I wanted to be able to give each of you a doll that can help you when the problems seem too big, or too complicated, or you haven't had enough life experience yet to help you know which path to take. And I wanted to take all my life experience and all the things I've learned and all my love for you and find some way to put those in a little package that you could carry around with you, and have with you all the time.

There are important things that come up in our lives—special occasions when we really wish our parents were with us. Special birthdays, graduating from high school, getting our driver's license, getting married, getting engaged, having our first baby. And so I've written you letters telling you how I feel about those important times and talking to you about what it was like for me when those things happened to me. And I've chosen little presents for you to mark those occasions, so you'll know that I was think-ing about you. It's awful that I can't be there, but at least you'll know that you filled my thoughts every moment, every moment. And that I didn't leave you without a fight.

Sometimes she looked directly into the camera; other times her gaze would drift up and away as she searched for words. She stayed quite still in her chair, a blanket over her lap. Occasionally she'd lift one hand to pull back a strand of hair the wind had tossed in her face. She spoke slowly and carefully, with the slight melodic lilt I re-membered from when we were younger. She must have imagined we would still be children, instead of teenagers, when we first watched this. In the background of the video, I heard the wind chimes hang-ing by the back door, the same few notes over and over, never re-solving into melody or meaning. Sitting on the bed all these years later, I could hear the same wind chimes blowing in the breeze out-side.

I have regrets that I put so much of our family life on hold while I was trying to save my life. I guess I only regret it because it seems that it hasn't worked. If it had worked it would have been worth every minute of discomfort and every bit of sacrifice. Being on that program, trying to fight my cancer often left me irritable and grumpy and feeling crummy. And I would try so hard to be patient and kind and calm and then suddenly—bang—I would get so cross because I felt so awful and I just was hanging on for dear life and sometimes it scared me, and I bet sometimes it scared you too. And I wish I could take back those years and make them different, but I can't. You need to know the truth. I haven't been all goodness and light all this time.

My mother's face crumpled, and she began to cry. I sank down into the pillows, as if they could shield me from what was happening in the video. I felt the same impulse I'd experienced watching horror films, to place my fingers over my eyes and peer between them, poised to snap them shut. Something was rending apart inside me. It was clear, in the rawness, the now barely concealed desperation of the woman on the screen, that the letters inside the cardboard chest were not the work of someone resigned to her death, but of someone still struggling, with all her might, to overcome it. She was only forty-four, I realized with a jolt, and facing down the end of her life. Even as a years-old echo, it was unbearable. Across the room, I heard Jamie begin quiet, gasping sobs. I couldn't even tell whether I was crying anymore; I only knew that huge bolts of energy were passing through me, as if I were standing at the center of a lightning storm.

This past summer we've really talked about the fact that I have a terminal illness, a life-threatening illness, and that the odds weren't very good that I was going to be able to stay with you much longer.

I'm not sure when it's going to be best for you to see this. Maybe it would be better for you to watch this before I die, maybe while I'm ill, or maybe it's gonna be better for you to wait. You and Daddy'll have to decide what makes the most sense to you.

But dying is hard work. It's real hard work. It's a lot like being born, I think. To leave our bodies. It's gonna be absolutely unbearable for me to have to leave you. And I suspect that's going to make dying very difficult for me because I don't wanna go any sooner than I have to. But when the time comes, and I need to turn inside, I don't want you to think I'm turning away from you. It's just that one goes on, I think, quite a profound journey when one is getting ready to leave this world and to go to the next world. It takes a lot of concentration. And a time will come when I need to turn way deep inside. And it will help me a lot to know that you're willing and ready to let me go.

And, Jamie and Gwenny, I think it was a very wise and mature choice that you made when you decided to be with Granny Liz after she'd died. I was very proud of you. And I think it was a very good preparation for what we'll need to face. I'd never been with a person who'd died either. And it was such a revelation to me. I really understood that we're not our bodies. Instantly, after Granny Liz died, there was this feeling that her true self was in her spirit and that her spirit left her body behind. I could feel her presence with me all the time I was washing her and dressing her and looking after her and getting her ready. I could feel her in the room with me. And I think that's going to help you think about what it's going to be like when I die. Because the minute—the instant after I die— you'll know, you'll just know, that I'm not my body—that my spirit really has been released and that I can be with you in a different way.

The video was nearly an hour long. It had clearly been recorded over several sessions, and the footage later cut together. In certain sections she was composed, but in others she wept so hard she could scarcely get her words out. As the minutes ticked by, Jamie and I slid down deeper and deeper into our seats. Our combined sadness built up in heaps and drifts around us, filling the room. We were both lying down by the end, spent.

If nothing else, I want to leave you with the knowledge that you have the right to the happiest, best, longest life that you can possibly give yourselves. Nothing could make me happier than knowing you've gone on to make happy lives for yourselves. That would be the very, very, very best thing that you could do in my memory. That would make me be able to face this better than anything. Because that's all I really long for—is for the two of you to have happy, full lives doing work that gives you pleasure, having relationships that give you joy. And I hope that—if you choose to be parents—that you'll have the deep, deep pleasure and wonder of having your own children to love the way I love you.

Her face froze on the screen; then the plinking music returned, then static. For a few seconds, the only sounds in the room were our heaving, shuddering breaths. Then we looked at each other, and burst into exhausted, hysterical laughter. It bubbled up from the very bottoms of our emotional barrels, and we writhed and groaned, as though movement and sound could exorcise the feeling from our bodies.

There was a strange sort of clamor going on in my chest, a bird caught in a snare. Our mother had spoken to us many times about death, but never with this degree of clarity or directness. We had never let her. I had always derailed the conversation with jokes or tantrums, and Jamie had always fallen asleep. She couldn't say the words to us, so she'd said them to the camera. She had imagined we might watch this tape sometime before her death, but I would never have been able to sit through it. Despite what she said about not being "all goodness and light," in my memory she had always given me her softness, her hope, her resilience. The tape contained one small glimpse of her pain, her anger, her despair.

"Oh, man," Jamie said, tears of laughter mixing with the ones already on his cheeks.

"I know," I said, "that was the heaviest thing I've ever seen."

We did not watch the other videos in the stack. We put them back in the fireproof safe and shut its door. We wouldn't open it again for another seven years.

F ifteenth birthday:

This coral necklace was brought back from Hong Kong by my father and [stepmother] and given to me for Christmas one year. It will suit you so much better than it ever suited me.

Though my mother and I attended the same high school, her student photo appears in only a single edition of the yearbook. At fifteen, skinny and freckled, she lived for a year in San Francisco while Granny Liz attended the Art Institute to earn her MFA. She returned as a sophomore, and can be found, smiling placidly, in the pages of the *Santa Rosa High School Echo* from 1968. By the time the 1969 issue went to print, she was gone.

Decades later, while working on this book, I would walk into the school guidance counselor's office and request a copy of her student files. Miraculously, they still had them. My mother had left the school long before anything was digitized, but a kind lady with a laminated lanyard around her neck pulled a thick manila folder from a back room and powered up the photocopier. My mother's student file outlined a brief but colorful tenure. Her grades were not the steady stream of As she had expected, and received, from Jamie and me, but a mix of Bs and Cs, a D in algebra, and another in driver's ed. She'd pulled a few As in English and history. There was a suspension, following repeated reprimands for breaking the dress code (Uncle Q explained that she had insisted on wearing an old blanket, with a hole in the middle, like a poncho). The file also contained two handwritten notes, one from my mother and one from Granny Liz, insisting that she had had nothing to do with what they referred to as "the unfortunate incident." This "incident" was still the stuff of

Santa Rosa High School legend when I began there, more than three decades later.

In 1969, a small band of students, my mother among them, printed and distributed a single issue of a "literary magazine," a handful of stapled pages containing one short story, a poem, a comic, and a letter from the editors. Antiwar sentiment on campus was in crescendo, and the theme of the magazine was coerced patriotism and censorship. The poem was the problem. At first glance, it appeared to be a sappy, badly written, over-the-top ode to SRHS as a great American institution; but if you took the first letter of each line and put them together, it read: S-H-I-T-O-N-Y-O-U-F-A-S-C-I-S-T-P-I-G-D-U-E-Y. Mr. Duey was the principal. My mother was only officially credited with cowriting the comic that appeared on the very back page, a fairly innocuous series of panels in which a group of bugs is trampled by a stampeding ogre. In the final frame, the bugs lie broken on the ground. *There is nothing so final as feet,* reads the thought bubble above their antennaed heads. In their letters, she and Granny Liz both claimed that, though my mother knew about the poem, she had been told it wouldn't be included in the magazine. Family opinion remains split on whether or not they were telling the truth. Their letters also imply that this was not my mother's first brush with the school's disciplinary apparatus.

Sometime after this infraction, at the age of seventeen, my mother left high school for good. Her records show that she later took classes at the UC Berkeley extension school, and petitioned the high school to issue her a diploma, but it's unclear whether her request was ever granted. She did not attend graduation. Instead, she packed a backpack and flew to Europe to join a marine archaeological expedition with her boyfriend, a PhD student she'd met while helping dig up shards of Chinese pottery from an old Spanish shipwreck near Point Reyes. Later she would follow the boyfriend to UC Santa Cruz, for her undergraduate work.

My favorite item in her student file was a letter from Principal Duey, apparently recommending her for some position.

> Kristina Mailliard, a junior at Santa Rosa High School, is a very intelligent young lady who expresses herself clearly and ably. She shows more than usual dissatisfaction with "the status quo," and with a directness that is quite unusual intends to effect change. Largely because of her own enthusiasm and interest, she has been able to get started a Student Federation on our campus; she has been able to hold this organization together largely by her own efforts to date, as the interest on the part of the students has been rather mild. Kristina is highly purposeful—what she intends, that she performs. It is my opinion that she would be, if chosen for the position, a dynamic, contributing member of the organization; there is no doubt that she would make her presence and ideas felt.

I arrived at SRHS with none of my mother's rebellious spirit, a rule follower through and through. By fifteen, I was taller than nearly every boy in my class, I had braces (for the second time!), and I belonged to a tight circle of rule-following friends.

The spring of my freshman year there was a dance, and I chose my dress specifically to match the coral necklace my mother had picked for my birthday. The necklace was beautiful, a soft ethereal pink, but more than that, it was the first thing I'd found in the chest that I could imagine wearing out into the world. I went to the dance with my pack of friends, boys and girls, and we bobbed awkwardly to Nickelback, Vanessa Carlton, and Maroon 5.

Suddenly, in the press of bodies, I felt something snap at the back of my neck, and heard the gentle rattle of tiny beads on the gymnasium floor. My whole body went cold. The music thudded on. I felt one bead, no bigger than a grain of rice, lodge itself between my instep and the sole of my silver sandal. Frantically I bent beneath the forest of twisting bodies, trying to gather as many of the beads as I could before they vanished, ground into powder against the shiny surface. I pressed the broken strands of the necklace hard against my chest with one hand, while with the other I felt for the little skittering granules, squatting in the dark between the pairs of stamping feet. They were so small, so numerous, and each one felt like a rebuke. As I reached among the dancers, my grip on the necklace slipped, and more pink beads poured from my chest to the floor. I knelt among them, stifling the urge to flip every switch on the long bank that controlled the overhead lights.

I felt a hand on my shoulder, and a friend asked what was wrong. She looked down at me, concerned, half her face draped in shadow. I opened my mouth, then closed it. In the space of a second, my fear for the necklace was overshadowed by my fear of anyone finding out what had happened to it. I couldn't explain what I'd done, that I'd brought something so precious into the scrum of my teenage world, and that the world had broken it. I hadn't told any of my friends where the necklace had come from, so they didn't know it was special. The people who knew its story—my father, an aunt, a godmother—could never find out it had broken. If no one but me knew both pieces of information, the catastrophe would not really have happened.

"Nothing," I said, "I thought I dropped something."

I stood, gripping the remains of the necklace in my hand.

"Bathroom!" I called to the silhouettes around me, and wove my way toward a neon-lighted exit.

. . .

My mother used to tell me a story about a day when Granny Liz's father, divorced from my great-grandmother and legally barred from entering their house, burst into the front hall and found her there alone. She was a child of six or seven, and he swept her up in his arms. At this point in the story, I always imagined my great-grandfather must have smelled like the oil paints that he spent all day working into canvases, coaxing them into layers of shadow and light. He set his daughter down and gave her a little chocolate man wrapped in silver foil, then said, "Don't tell your mother I was here," and raced away. Granny Liz ate the chocolate and then wept because the little man was all she had left of her father, and now it was gone. She'd used the gift as he'd intended, but destroyed it all the same.

My father married Shirlee the summer after my freshman year, in the Episcopal church where I'd been baptized. I wore a pink flowered skirt and a pink sweater and held a bunch of pink peonies in my lap in the first pew. It was a bright June day, but the hundred-year-old church remained dark and cool. I sat between Jamie, wearing a coat and tie, and my father's father, who had flown over from England. Granddad had visited California every few years when we were small, but he was in his eighties now, and came only for things like weddings and funerals.

The day before, Granddad had asked me to take him to the cemetery and show him the spot where my mother was buried. Her headstone sat at the foot of an oak tree whose trunk had split more than a century ago and grown up double, like two trees joined at the roots. I'd planted a ring of amaryllis belladonna over the place where we'd sunk the ceramic vase containing her ashes, but there were no flowers yet, only a mass of glossy green leaves. Granddad and I sat together on a low concrete wall across from her marker, looking at her name etched in granite.

As long as I'd known him, Granddad had had wispy gray hair, very thin on top, prominent ears, and black-rimmed glasses. His scalp and hands were spotted with age. When he smiled, he looked exactly like my father.

"Remarkable woman," he said, reading my mother's name.

My grandmother had died when I was two, and Granddad had never remarried. He lived alone in a small house at the top of a valley, in a little village south of London. He played golf and bridge and took care of the flowers and shrubs that Granny Jean had planted. In that moment, I wished my father could be like that, eternally loyal to the memory of my mother. How could he be ready to move on with life, when I still felt so hungry for the past?

"Remarkable woman," Granddad said again. We cleared some fallen leaves from my mother's plot, and polished the dusty stone with handfuls of our clothes.

My father and Shirlee's wedding reception took place on the grounds of the mansion where the movie *Pollyanna* had been filmed four decades before. The current owners, our neighbors, were renovating the house, but offered them the use of the expansive lawn. Throughout the day, people sought me out and hugged me tightly. They were the same people who'd hugged me three years earlier, after my mother's memorial service—my aunts and uncles, my godparents, my mother's friends—and they said the same kinds of things they'd said then: "Call anytime. We're here if you need us. She would be so proud of you." Later, my father, Jamie, and I stood for photos with Shirlee and David, a portrait of our new, blended family. Looking at the pictures later, I was almost surprised to see my own image show up in the frame; I'd barely felt like I was there at all.

Even though there was no package, no letter for this day, my thoughts drifted to the cardboard chest and the thick envelope with *Gwenny's Engagement* written across it. At that moment, I felt I never wanted to attend another wedding in my life. Yet at the same time, I craved all the words I knew were packed into that envelope, waiting for me, meant to address the questions a daughter asks her mother on the day she decides to join her life to another's. I let my thoughts wander out through my bedroom window, and down the tree-lined street. I let them take me back to the cemetery where I had walked with Granddad the day before. In my mind, I took the path, thick with oak leaves, to my mother's grave, and laid a bunch of pink peonies down on the earth.

At first, the changes were small. I'd come home to a kitchen that looked somehow different. It would take me a few minutes, or hours, to realize that the vegetable clock in the kitchen had been replaced by one with numbers, or that one of Granny Liz's etchings had been swapped with a painting of water lilies. But as the summer sweltered on, the house was steadily emptied of all evidence that another woman, another family, had ever lived there. The *Alice in Wonderland* playing cards and the pink flamingos vanished from the entryway, the *Wizard of Oz* illustrations vacated their walls, and one night, a few weeks after the wedding, we sat down to dinner in a dining room utterly devoid of origami fish. One day I came home from school to the smell of wet paint, and realized that the red living room was no longer red. The alterations were not discussed beforehand. I tried to become more vigilant about noticing my surroundings, as if the force of my attention could protect the things I saw. I felt a new anxiety about objects, about what their presence or absence meant to a space.

"Just please don't get rid of the geese," I begged one evening. For years a dish towel rack shaped like the heads of three Canada geese had jutted from the wall by the kitchen sink.

"You're not very observant," Shirlee said, pointing to the stainless steel ring she'd already installed in its place.

Another day, I wanted to bake my mother's oatmeal cookies and couldn't find the little recipe box, shaped like a log cabin, that Jamie had made for me all those Christmases ago. I looked on high shelves and in low cupboards and even in the attic, where many of my mother's things had begun to accumulate. Finally I asked my father about it, and he promised to look too. Later that night, he came into my room to tell me Shirlee had accidentally thrown it away. I felt the loss of that little box even more deeply than the destruction of the coral necklace. To me, it represented both my mother, through the recipes, and my brother, through the craftsmanship. I missed them both every single day I woke up in the house without them, and this one disappearance came to stand, in my mind, for everything else that was vanishing around me.

David came to live with us. He still spent time with his father, but our house was closer to school. He needed a room, and so my mother's old bedroom was emptied of its boxes of embroidery floss, its sets of Dickens and Agatha Christie, its books on philosophy and parenting and death. The carved oak bed frame was replaced with one made of pine. The La-Z-Boy armchair went to the curb. I knew that David deserved a space of his own, but I couldn't help grieving the loss of that quiet room where I'd spent so many afternoons, and I couldn't quell the panic I felt every time I came home to a slightly different version of the house I'd once known so well.

Sixteenth birthday:

You and Daddy chose this for me, and I wore it all the time until I began spending so much time in hospitals where you aren't allowed to wear jewelry. You begged me to leave it to you, and so I have. With all my love.

xox Mommy

My father said that one day, when suitors came asking to take me out, he would present them with a handful of identical white zircons and ask them to pick out the one real diamond among the fakes. He actually purchased the gems, which he kept in a little enameled box, along with a square of green jeweler's cloth on which to spread them.

"Which is the real one?" I asked, squinting.

"None of them," he said. "They're all fake. I only want to see how carefully they look."

I rolled my eyes, and put the sparkling stones back in the box.

"You're the real diamond," my father said, putting a hand on my shoulder. "It's important they know that."

But my father never got the chance to administer the test of the stones. My first boyfriend did not come in through the front door, asking for a date. Rather, he revealed himself by degrees.

I'd known Zach since the third grade. Back then, he had an unusually large head, with thick brown hair cut into a neat bowl and big blue-gray eyes with long dark lashes. He was small for his age, only reaching my shoulder, and would make me laugh by emptying out his large canvas backpack and pulling it over himself until he was just a pair of feet walking around the blacktop. He spoke with a slight stutter that came and went like weather, pronounced on some days, barely there on others. I liked Zach because he could do one hundred Fast Facts arithmetic problems in four minutes, while it always took me five.

In elementary school, Zach would invite me over to his house to play video games. We would sit together on the old couch in his basement, which was covered in a blue cotton sheet. My brother and I had grown up playing computer games, but we'd never owned a Nintendo. I died instantly the first few times I tried to pilot Mario through his two-dimensional world of pipes; after that, I mostly watched as Zach made him leap from block to block, crushing turtles and mushrooms and collecting shiny gold coins along the way. I loved it the same way I loved to watch Jamie play Warcraft. There was something in the side-by-side of it, our attention on the same brightly lit thing. I imagined my thoughts could help him lift Mario over a long chasm, save him from the zing of a turtle shell.

The summer between our freshman and sophomore years of high school, Zach grew taller and taller, until we were looking directly into each other's eyes. We often walked home from school together, and most days we would pause when we reached my driveway, lost in conversation. We were both members of the debate club, and I admired the way he got hold of a single question—Is it ethical to eat meat? How should college admissions work? Does God exist?—and worked it like a bird with a seed, trying to crack it open, looking for an answer that felt final. We would take opposing positions on a topic and argue ourselves to a standstill, then switch sides and keep going. We argued until we had to sit down on the rough concrete of the driveway, until our throats began to hurt. I don't remember when the conversations moved from the driveway and up into my bedroom; I only remember that we kissed for the first time sitting side by side on my bed. It felt as though all the words that had poured from our mouths had always been leading us here.

For my sixteenth birthday, Zach and I went with a group of friends to see *Finding Neverland* at the local multiplex. We bought Dr Peppers, supersized bags of popcorn covered in gooey butter-flavored oil, and boxes of frozen Junior Mints. When the previews started, Zach and I licked our fingers clean and held hands.

"Happy birthday," he whispered into my ear as the theater went dark, and I felt the whole left side of my body turn to static.

That morning I'd pulled the small triangular amethyst on its fine gold chain from the chest.

I remembered buying the necklace with my father when I was seven or eight. I'd saved up my allowance, and when the woman in the jewelry store told us the price, I thought the necklace cost a dollar and change, and eagerly unzipped my little denim shoulder bag. My father and the woman both laughed. They explained that the necklace cost one *hundred* and seventy-five dollars. My cheeks burned as I zipped my bag closed again. My father put his hand on my shoulder and said he would take care of it. I loved the necklace, but I was sad not to have bought it myself. For years afterward, I would pull the necklace from her jewelry box and roll the little triangular stone between my fingers. I liked the way it was fixed on its chain, always occupying the exact center. I liked the way it nestled perfectly in the indentation between my mother's collarbones.

There was also an extra present to celebrate my driver's license, a little leather change purse on a key ring, for parking quarters, stamped with my initials. The note read:

> Gwenny DRIVING ... Holy smokes! How exciting!! Please
> be safe, wear your seatbelt and drive with caution.
> xoxox Mommy

On the morning of my birthday, I'd gone to the DMV before

school and gotten a license to go with my own thirdhand blue Volvo. The leather purse dangled from my car keys as I drove myself to school that morning. My friends and I squealed over the battered sedan as if it were a Ferrari.

If my mother had been too impatient to wait for her graduation day, I wished mine would never come. At sixteen I had a boyfriend, my own car, and four spectacular friends. Margaret was an artist and a true romantic, though she hid it well beneath a tough, joking exterior she'd developed growing up with two brothers. Erica was a choir kid who wore enormous sunglasses, drove a white Mercedes, and always smelled like vanilla. Emma subscribed to fashion magazines, owned CDs by obscure bands, and bought her clothes from American Apparel in San Francisco. Freesia was involved with nearly every committee and club on campus, and also competed on a synchronized swimming team. She seemed to share my nostalgia for the past and loved taking snapshots of the rest of us, developing them later in the darkroom of her photography class. The five of us, along with Zach, called ourselves the Sensational Six, and they became my escape from all the sadness and anxiety I now felt at home. We spent most weekends squashed into a single car, tracing the tidy grid of our small city, learning its shape, seeking its hidden spaces. Our favorite of these was a hilltop overlooking the city's south side, accessed by a perilously steep and winding road. The engine of my ancient Volvo always roared and whined in protest as we inched our way up.

"I think I can, I think I can," everyone would chant, as I leaned hard on the accelerator.

At the top, we'd hop a low fence, ignoring a NO TRESPASSING sign with the brazenness I'd learned from my father (my rule-following was limited to school). The site had been under a development contract for years, but no construction ever seemed to begin. We'd make our way to our favorite lookout in starlight, sometimes bringing a plastic water bottle half-full of tequila or vodka to pass around, taking little sips, making it last.

Our city spread beneath us, made of glowing streetlights and veins of sparkling traffic. To the southeast I could pick out Our Lady of the Washing Machine Agitator, as Granny Liz used to call the Catholic church with the tall white spire. Directly below us spun the pink neon sign of the Flamingo Hotel, where friends and family had stayed when they came to visit my mother and our house was too full of guests to hold any more. I did not know the names of the constellations in the night sky overhead, but the ones made by the landmarks in the streets below me were as familiar to me as my own name.

"Look," I'd say, pointing, "we grew up in the best place in the world. Why would anyone want to leave?"

In the ninth grade, I'd found my place among the drama kids, and my school schedule included two hours of acting class every day, with extra time after school if we were rehearsing a play. Our coursework was a pastiche of Stanislavsky, Michael Chekhov, Meisner, Laban, Uta Hagen. We studied "affective memory," the technique of using real events from our pasts to access a fictional character's feelings. We worked on achieving spontaneity through repetition exercises, trying to sweep away the "acting" and find something more authentic. We practiced "endowing" objects with emotional significance, so that we might live on a stage set the same way we lived in our real homes. When I stepped through the heavy metal door into that dusty, windowless black box filled with colored light, I felt I was leaving high school behind altogether, and making art as vital as any in the grown-up world.

For many actors, the pleasure in the work comes from transforming into someone else, but for me, the pleasure, the relief, always came from the opportunity to become more myself. I rarely spoke with my peers, even my closest friends, about my mother's death. Most of the kids I went to school with had never experienced death so close at hand, and had never had to develop an emotional vocabulary for it. I could see a door slide closed behind their eyes when I brought it up. They didn't intend to be unkind; they simply had no idea what I was talking about. But within the theater walls, characters contended with challenges far greater than anything I had ever experienced. Women were beaten by their domestic partners and took their own lives. Parents lost their children in accidents or wars. People starved and bled and were banished, and we were asked to feel every bit of it. The emotions I struggled to control at home and in every other context of my life were welcomed in this one. Onstage, they were assets. The first time I performed a monologue and wept, and looked up to find the class crying with me, I felt I'd been given the keys to my emotional freedom. I could communicate the way I felt through other people's words, if not through my own.

At age sixteen, Tippy, an extremely healthy dog all her life, began a steep decline. Her back legs grew stiff with arthritis, her two different-colored eyes both filmed over with cataracts, and she lost control of her bowels. At the vet's suggestion, we picked a day on the calendar. It turned out to be one of her good days, and as we lifted her into the car, she wagged the white-tipped tail that had inspired her name, as if to make us doubt our decision.

In the waiting room at the vet's office hung a series of charts showing different dog breeds arranged by size. My father and I made a game of pointing to them and guessing what they were, making each other laugh. Shirlee, who had been steadily weeping since we got in the car, looked horrified, and my father and I tried to control our twitching mouths. I found it frustrating that her sadness about the dog filled up so much emotional space. Neither my father nor I responded to Tippy's impending death with tears. Somehow they would have felt insufficient. There'd been other pets over the years—a second parakeet, a hamster I had shamefully neglected—but Tippy had always been there. I couldn't remember a time without her.

I had never experienced the moment of life leaving flesh. As Tippy lay on the metal table, I placed both my hands on her black fur. *She's about to learn the secret,* I thought, *of what it's like to die.* Closing my eyes, I willed some small sliver of the experience to be revealed to me, some glimpse of where Davey, Granny Liz, and my mother had all gone. Instead, I felt only a slight shudder as the needle went into her paw, then stillness.

The next day I called Jamie from the privacy of my parked car to tell him Tippy was gone.

"Oh," he said, the single syllable managing to convey a kaleidoscope of sadness, gratitude, and acceptance, the emotional stew of losing an old friend after a long life. Then, "Actually, I have something to tell you, too."

Once, when my brother was very angry with me, he took his temper out on my bedroom. He was about twelve, and I had done something truly egregious, though now I have no idea what it was. I came through the door, damp and briny from a dip in the pool, a towel around my waist, and paused inside the threshold, dimly aware that something had happened. A few books lay on the floor at the foot of my bookcase, the bed covers were flung back, and a small doll's rocking chair rested upside down on its wooden arms, though the doll herself sat nearby, untouched. The room looked as though a very small earthquake had lazily shaken a few objects loose before subsiding. I puzzled over the disturbances, then walked back out to the pool where Jamie's dark head still bobbed in the deep end.

"Were you in my room earlier?"

"I'm so sorry," he said at once, paddling toward the metal ladder at the pool's edge. "I'll put it all back right now."

I'd told this story to Zach, who also had older siblings, and it had made him laugh. After that, I told it wherever I wanted to illustrate the dynamic between my older brother and me. In some versions, I emphasized the contrast between Jamie's stoicism and my volatility. Other times, it was a story about Jamie's social anxiety, his difficulty expressing anger or frustration or standing up for himself. Both of these interpretations contained truth, but neither of them got to the root of why I continued to tell the story so often. I told it because recounting this small anecdote filled me with such excruciating feelings of tenderness for my brother that I could have sat down and wept. It was a story about how precious, how dear this person was to me, and why I wanted to protect him from the careless buffeting of the world with everything I had.

Jamie was a senior in college, and his girlfriend, Sally, had graduated the year before. They were twenty-two and twenty-three, and they were pregnant. They didn't know it yet, but they were having twins.

As he spoke the words to me over the phone—"broken condom," "morning-after pill," "her choice"—I saw him at twelve years old, guiltily turning my doll's rocking chair right side up and placing her on its wicker seat. The boy in the memory looked so very young, but only ten years separated him from the man on the phone. Fear gathered behind my breastbone as I thought about what this would mean for the years ahead. It meant that Jamie would not come back to California after graduation. Sally's family lived in North Carolina, so he would likely move east for good. I leaned my head against the car window. I felt indescribably lonely, as if everyone I loved were leaving me behind. It was my old battle with time. No matter how hard I wished it, the world would not stand still.

"I need a favor," Jamie was saying through the phone.

"Of course," I said. "Anything."

"I need you to go to my room and open the chest. I know there's a box with an engagement ring. I need you to find it and tell me if it's a good ring."

Jamie's chest had remained in his childhood bedroom all through college. He opened his gifts when he came home during summers, or for Christmases. Sometimes he forgot to open them at all. He didn't seem to need them the same way I did. Maybe he'd absorbed more of the living woman than I had. Jamie and I never discussed the gifts and letters we found inside our chests. I hardly discussed them with anyone. To me, they felt intensely private, and Jamie was such a private person to begin with that I just assumed he wouldn't want to talk about it. Apart from the time I'd tried to convince him to take his eighteenth-birthday present to South America, I'd never seen the inside of his chest, and even though I had his permission, I still felt a small thrill of the forbidden as I entered Jamie's room and lifted the wicker lid.

The contents were spare—Jamie had put more birthdays behind him—but the remaining packages looked just like mine, a collection of small, colorful boxes tied with ribbon and labeled with white tags. I quickly spotted the word *Engagement* printed on one tag, and pulled it out.

The ring was a thin gold band, set with a round solitaire diamond. The note said the ring had once belonged to our father's grandmother. I snapped a photo with the little camera on my flip phone, and texted it to Jamie along with the caption: IT'S A GOOD RING.

On the morning of my high school graduation, I felt as though someone had filled my limbs with sand. This, I felt, was the end of everything. In a few months, all my beloved friends would scatter like leaves, attending colleges spread down the state and across the country. Zach had secured early admission to Stanford, while I was headed east.

During the previous fall, I had sleepwalked through the entire college selection process, sending out my applications as if I were throwing darts at a numberless board. I had no idea where I wanted to go to school, because I didn't want to go anywhere. I'd transferred all the love I'd once felt for my house onto the surrounding city, and I wanted to stay. I requested my transcripts and wrote my essays and filled out financial forms, all in a state of horrified dissociation. My father, unfamiliar with the American university system, had mostly left me to it, and without the help of one of my parents' friends, an attorney who took my education very seriously, I might never have applied anywhere at all. For no particular reason, I'd settled on a small liberal arts college in Boston called Tufts. When I emailed to tell them I was coming, I felt as if I'd found myself in the middle of a busy street wearing my pajamas, waking from one nightmare into another.

I rolled myself out of bed and onto the floor, then crawled on all fours over to the cardboard chest. I tugged it toward me by one brass handle and sat cross-legged in front of it. Opening the chest was, by now, a familiar ritual, like lighting birthday candles, or placing ornaments on a tree. I flipped back both the latches at once and enjoyed the rattling sound of the metal, amplified by the hollow drum of the box. I placed my hands on either side of the domed lid and lifted, relishing the slight resistance of the laminated edges sticking together. Two sets of metal hinges unfolded silently, propping the lid open.

Over the years, I'd worked my way through the topmost layer of packages, and the ones that were left fit together less snugly. Beneath the black sketchbook, a few little boxes had fallen on their sides. Some of the curly ribbon had gone flat, some of the tags were a little bent. The box marked *High School Graduation* was a flat rectangle, larger than most of the others; instead of metal or cardboard, it was made of blue velvet. I pulled off the ribbon and ran my hands over the soft, short pile of the material. The case snapped open on tiny hinges to reveal a string of milky saltwater pearls. The note card directed me to page 22 in the sketchbook.

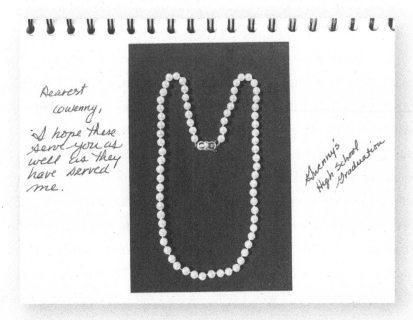

Dearest
Gwenny,

I hope these
serve you as
well as they
have served
me.

Gwenny's
High School Graduation

There seemed to be a tradition in my family that when the girls graduated from high school they received a string of pearls (or at least Antoinette did). Well, perhaps because I chose to stay in public high school against my father's wishes, or perhaps because I skipped my senior year, my string of pearls never arrived so . . . after I graduated from business school I went on a brief adventure to Japan and brought home some pearls which I had strung at Shreve's in San Francisco. A graduation string of pearls at last. I have worn them often—wedding, both your and Jamie's christenings—at all important occasions.

xox Mommy

The pearls made a sound like a tiny maraca as I pulled them from their case. I ran my fingers along them one bead at a time, trying to slow my breathing. They were so beautiful, and they were no use to me at all. I don't know what I'd hoped the package would contain. A trapdoor that would transport me into another reality, where I would never have to leave home? But so often my mother had anticipated what I needed before I knew it myself.

I sat on the floor of my room, in the house where my mother had died, in the city where she had lived. A line traced from her childhood home to her elementary school, her middle school, her high school, and finally to the place where she was buried would encompass just forty city blocks. That had been the backdrop of her life, as it had been the backdrop of mine. Yet at seventeen she had leapt at the opportunity for adventure, seizing it with both hands, so eager to leave home she hadn't even waited for a diploma. She had expanded the scope of her life, and only returned to the place where she began in order to have her children. I wanted to skip the entire adventure and stay right where I was. I'd hoped the graduation package would offer me a way to stay; instead, my mother had given me the thing that *she* had wished for at my age: this handful of pearls, a formal acknowledgment that she was ready to go.

Graduation was a half day of school for seniors. I spent the morning with the Sensational Six, writing in each other's yearbooks and making plans for summer. At lunchtime we drove to our favorite Mexican restaurant and crammed into a booth meant for four. I sat on Zach's lap. We lined up the little plastic cups holding different salsas: green, red, extra spicy, pico de gallo. We ordered nachos for the table. Margaret and Erica shared a burrito. Freesia drank an horchata. It was exactly the same as the other hundred times we'd eaten there. I wanted to hold us all around that table, and never let a single one of my friends stand up. I was already wearing the silky blue sundress I'd picked out for under my graduation robes. A bit of salsa dropped onto the hem, soaking into the fibers before I could wipe it away.

The sun beat down on the football field as our graduating class of five hundred sat down on the rows of black folding chairs. In accordance with tradition, a few students had hidden inflatable beach balls under their robes, which they blew up and began to bat around overhead. Each time one appeared, the assistant principal would run onto the field to confiscate it. After a few minutes, another would float up over the crowd in its place. My friends all sat rows away from me, scattered throughout the alphabet.

I'd heard somewhere that pearls absorbed the oils from human skin, and that it strengthened them. Unworn pearls could become dry and brittle and break. I rolled the smooth spheres against my chest with my fingers. Each time my mother had worn them, they would have absorbed a tiny bit of her. She'd never sat on this field among her classmates, batting beach balls and listening to the principal drone into the microphone. She'd missed her own graduation, but some small essence, distilled from her body, was present at this one, in the pearls, in me. When I heard my name I stood and walked across the short green Astroturf, reaching out my hand for the small prop scroll of paper the principal lifted from the pile of half a thousand identical cylinders. As I walked, I imagined the girl from the black-and-white photographs accompanying me, thirty-seven years late, over that momentous childhood-ending line.

Jamie was married that summer in Durham, North Carolina. I and the other bridesmaids wore red. The ceremony was outdoors, and tiny gnats kept biting my ankles as I stood in the grass, holding my bouquet of gerberas and waiting for the bride to walk between the rows of folding chairs. She looked beautiful, and very pregnant, as she glided toward us.

The wedding dinner was barbecue. I wandered among the tables with the glass of champagne I'd been allowed for the occasion. Our mother's large family, and our father's small one, had gathered to wish Jamie well on this next chapter of his life. In the presence of so many people I associated with my mother, it was easy to imagine that she was there too, somewhere in the crowd, perhaps managing the catering or the music behind the scenes.

For several childhood summers, when I was too homesick to sign up for camp, even the kind that only met during the day and let you go home at night, my mother had solved the problem by creating her own summer camp which she ran out of our backyard. She named it the Pocket School. She convinced a handful of local parents to send their children to our house each day, and with the money they paid her she hired a clown, a naturalist, and a storyteller. The clown, whose professional name was Hoopla and who had once worked for Ringling Bros., taught us face painting, juggling, and how to walk on stilts. The naturalist taught us to identify plants and birds, and took us on field trips to the Marin Headlands to look at trees and rock formations. The storyteller taught history and ancient myth.

One summer she hired a drama teacher who directed us in a play based on the stories of *The Fools of Chelm*, a collection of Yiddish folktales about a town full of fools who believe themselves very wise. Someone recorded a shaky home movie of this production, filmed over the heads of the thirty or so friends and family who assembled in the backyard to see our big performance at the end of the summer. In the bottom right corner of the frame stands my mother, watching from the very back of the audience. She wears a periwinkle-blue linen dress with a matching short-sleeved vest, and her hair is a dark, inch-long fuzz.

Onstage, Jamie, aged twelve, is playing a young man called Yossel, asking his mother for advice on how to speak to the woman he loves.

"It is simple, my boy," his mother, played by my friend Ella, assures him in a quavering old-womanish voice. "First you talk about love, then you talk about family, then you finish up with a little philosophy."

In the next scene, Jamie sits down to speak with his beloved, Sossel, and follows his mother's advice.

"Tell me, Sossel," he says, "do you love noodles?"

"Yes," Sossel replies, "I love noodles."

"And tell me, Sossel," he goes on, "do you have a brother?"

"No," she says, "I don't have a brother."

At this point, Jamie leaps up for a whispered aside to the audience: "This is going to be easier than I thought! I've already talked about love and family, now I'll finish up with a little philosophy."

Sitting back down beside Sossel, Jamie asks, "But tell me, Sossel, if you had a brother, would he love noodles?"

The audience loves the joke, and our mother laughs and claps along with everyone else as she watches her twelve-year-old son rehearse asking someone to marry him. Whenever I watch this part of the video I'm struck by the fact that somewhere, inside the house behind her, is a package with Jamie's name on it, already containing the diamond engagement ring, ready for when the time comes.

As I watched my brother cut his wedding cake, I wished I could do something, anything, to make the path ahead of him easier. I couldn't imagine having twins at the age of twenty-two. Even with all the support I knew he'd have, the support of all the people gathered in that room, I still worried. I wanted every good thing for him. For a moment, I thought I felt a glimmer of what our mother must have felt as she packed those chests: an overwhelming desire to comfort and protect. For a moment, I thought I might understand, just a little, what it was like to be her.

As summer waned, the song "Boston" by Augustana played over and over on the radio, making me break out in cold sweat each time as I fumbled to change the station. "I think I'll go to Boston," the stereo seemed to mock me, "I think I'll start a new life, where no one knows my name." The season seemed to last no time at all.

In the final weeks of August, the Sensational Six rented a beach house in Bodega Bay for a long weekend. The house cost $110 per night. Its wooden walls were weathered gray by the salt air, it had no potable water or insulation, and a single woodstove provided the only source of heat. Even in August, the Northern California evenings were chilly, and each morning we shivered in our pajamas, trying to reignite the dying coals from the previous night's fire.

We went for long walks on the foggy beach, wading up to our ankles in the frigid Pacific. We cooked simple meals, and tried not to burn the place down with the outdated oven. We stayed up late and got up late, and took naps in the front room where the walls were made of glass and the sun warmed it like a greenhouse. We decided we would come back to that house once a year, every year, for the rest of our lives.

I wrote down every detail of that weekend on ruled pages torn from someone's notebook. I wrote down the names of the people we were dating, and the schools where we were enrolled: a time capsule. I wrote the final sentences while everyone else was cleaning the dishes and taking out the trash. Then we all sat around the kitchen table and I read aloud the story of our weekend.

"So we'll remember," I said. "I mean, we're going to do this every year. If we don't write down the details, they'll all start to blur together."

We rolled up the pages and placed them in an empty pasta sauce jar and buried it under a hedge in front of the house. The next year, we would dig it up again.

Freesia was the first to leave, headed to school in New York. We all gathered at her house to say good-bye before her parents drove her to the airport. When the little gold Prius was packed and ready, she suddenly took off running down the street. The five of us ran after her, fanning out across the wide sweep of her cul-de-sac. We caught up with her on the corner, where her little street met the main road.

"I don't want to go!" she sobbed.

My heart throbbed in recognition, in relief. When the moment to part finally came, I wasn't the only one who wanted to run. We walked her back up the street in a kind of huddle, our arms tangled around her, our feet finding the same rhythm. I felt like a traitor as we delivered her back to her parents and put her in the car. I wanted to tell her she didn't have to go, that we could run away together, hide out the way we had when we were twelve and her parents had come to pick her up from my house, because we wanted to play a little longer. The five of us stood on the sidewalk and waved until she was out of sight. A few days later, Erica and Emma left for different schools in Southern California. Margaret would be staying in town to attend the local junior college before transferring, and Zach, bound for Stanford, had the latest start date of us all.

When it was my turn to leave, Zach drove me to the airport. I'd asked my father not to come because I was afraid, if he did,

I'd never get on the plane. Zach had to pull over on the freeway twice so I could vomit. I'd never felt so horribly alienated from my body, from myself, as though the arms holding my bags and the legs walking me through the sliding glass doors of the terminal belonged to someone else. At the threshold, I turned back for one more hug, and only realized I was crying when I saw the wetness smeared on Zach's face. He told me everything would be okay. I wanted to believe him.

I settled into my seat on the plane with a book, the latest in a British YA series I'd adored as a tween, a comfort read. The first two hours were uneventful, but somewhere over Nebraska I lost control of my breath.

At first I tried to hide the ragged gulps of air that forced their way in and out of my lungs, pulling the hot-pink hardback closer and closer to my face. Then little noises began to escape my mouth, tiny squeaks and chirps, like some small furry creature in distress. The woman in the next seat asked if I was all right. I nodded, unable to form words. Tears splattered onto my arms, chest, and lap. I folded myself into the extreme corner of my window seat, trying to tamp down whatever was bursting its way out of me.

My neighbor pressed the call button, and a few moments later a flight attendant appeared at the end of our row.

"She seems to be having a tough time," the woman next to me explained. "Could we get some water?"

"Sure," said the flight attendant. Then, to me: "Do you need anything else? Do you take any medication?"

I tried to communicate, through a series of hand gestures, that I was fine, that it would pass. In truth, I had no idea what was happening, or if it would pass, but I couldn't accept the help and sympathy these women offered. I was too humiliated. I was eighteen years old and on my way to college, but I suddenly felt just as I had when I was eight, lying on the floor of Becca's bedroom wishing my father would come pick me up.

For the last three hours of the flight to Boston, I sipped water, looked out the window, and tried to keep my breathing regular. An idea was slowly coming into focus. It was simple: I would not go to college. Somehow this had never occurred to me before. College had always seemed a horrible inevitability, like braces or a tetanus shot, something it was impossible to refuse. The thought of not going was like land beneath my thrashing feet.

I dialed my home number the moment I was off the jetway at Logan Airport.

"How was the flight?" my father asked from a continent away.

I told him I wasn't going to college. He told me that I was.

"Go find John," he said. "Go home with him, and we'll talk about this later."

My father had arranged for John, my mother's best friend from business school and my brother's godfather, to take me home for the night. He was a tall, powerfully built man with thinning hair and a round, cherubic face. I found him easily, and he folded me in large, comforting arms. He had four children of his own, two of them daughters.

"Welcome to Boston!" he said, and I burst into tears.

John took me to a burger joint where I managed to pick at a few french fries. My stomach felt like I had left it somewhere on the freeway in San Francisco.

"Well," he said, after I poured out my story, "it will probably take a day or two to get a flight back to California. Why don't you come home with me tonight, and tomorrow I'll take you to campus. You can just walk around and just see how it feels."

Just see how it feels.

I was six years old on a family ski trip to Lake Tahoe. My father had signed me up for skiing lessons, while he and Jamie hit the slopes. My mother had stayed at home. I begged my father not to leave me behind with the ski instructors and other unfamiliar children.

"How about you just stay for the morning?" he coaxed. "I'll come back at lunchtime and check on you. Just see how it feels."

I spent the morning learning to "pizza" my skis, and falling down a lot in the soft, powdery snow. At lunchtime we peeled off our parkas and ate grilled cheese sandwiches and Now and Laters in front of cartoons. I kept looking over my shoulder, waiting for my father to appear in the doorway, but he never came.

After lunch, as everyone prepared to go back outside, I approached one of the instructors and explained that I was only supposed to stay for the morning, that my father was coming to get me. "Can you call him? Maybe he forgot the time."

They patiently explained that if my father was on the slopes, there was no way to get in touch with him. It was 1995.

I refused to go back outside with the other kids, afraid my father would arrive after I left. One of the instructors had to sit with me all afternoon while I waited for him. When he finally appeared, I flung myself into his arms.

"Why didn't you come?" I wailed into his shoulder.

"I did," he assured me. "I poked my head in at lunchtime and you were having a good time, so I left."

I spent the night staring at the ceiling of John's youngest daughter's bedroom. I revisited my decision to go to Tufts, over and over, wondering how it had happened. It seemed as if someone else had made that choice, as if I had fallen asleep at the wheel of my life and woken suddenly to find myself thousands of miles off course.

"This is not my life," I whispered to myself, again and again.

It had been so much easier just to do what everyone else was doing than to consider another path. The problem wasn't Tufts, or Boston; the problem was that I had walked straight into my own worst nightmare (moving to the other side of the country) because I lacked the imagination to conceive of an alternative.

I looked around at another girl's teenage bedroom, at the photos of friends taped to her mirror, the dried corsage hanging from the corner of a bookshelf, the yearbooks stacked on the desk. Maybe, in a dorm room hundreds of miles away, she was also awake, homesick for this room and all its memories. But she had managed to leave home for a new adventure. My friends were managing it. I alone, it seemed, was incapable of taking this next step. At my age, my mother had already traveled to Europe on her own. If only I could have gone with her. I pictured the two of us walking in moonlight through the cobbled streets of some tiny Greek town, two girlfriends laughing on their way to beds in a hostel, casting matching shadows on the ground. I felt more alone than I had on the night she died, more alone than I'd ever felt in my life.

The next morning I managed to shower, but lacked the energy to dry my hair. I'd barely slept, but my fatigue went deeper than that. I felt like someone had wrung the life force from my body. John drove me to campus and walked with me across the emerald lawns. He suggested I go to the dorms and find my roommate; the idea made me want to evaporate into the bright late-August air.

From across the green expanse, a figure came running toward me, and I recognized a friend from high school.

"Hi!" Katie said, throwing her arms around me. "You look terrible."

"I know," I said. I was both happy to see a familiar face, and disappointed to be recognized when I so deeply wanted to be invisible.

"Come on"—she tugged my arm—"the matriculation ceremony is about to start."

I sat with Katie and the twelve hundred other freshmen entering the College of Arts and Sciences under a white pergola draped with greenery. I recited the oath of admission, my fingers crossed behind my back.

That evening I spoke with my father on the phone again, and begged him to let me come home. I could hear the frustration in his voice. This was the result, his tone seemed to suggest, of all the years he had picked me up from summer camps and slumber parties, all the years he had indulged my homesickness. He should have put his foot down earlier, and so he would put it down now. It never occurred to me to call my therapist from Boston. Judy, I felt, could not help me here. It would have been like phoning a therapist for help while standing on a sinking ship.

"When I rowed at university," my father was saying on the phone, "toward the end of a race my whole body would be exhausted. Everything hurt, and I didn't think I could last another second. Everything in me wanted to give up and rest. But I did keep going, because the boat was moving, and if your oar doesn't move, the water will take it. You keep pace with the person in front of you, and the person behind you, and the boat keeps moving forward. We're all capable of more than we think."

My father's enormous prize oars, inscribed with the names of everyone on his crew, hung in the front hall of our house. I understood the metaphor, but at the same time, I wondered, *How can you be sure your boat is pointed in the right direction?*

"You can do this, Gwenny," he said. And then, "You're your mother's daughter."

I felt as though I'd been slapped. My father rarely mentioned my mother. Since Shirlee had moved into the house, he hardly spoke her name. I would have loved to hear those words from him on a thousand other occasions, but now he'd used them to outmaneuver me. My arm felt suddenly limp. I let the phone fall on the seat beside me. I'd only been in Boston a couple days, and I already felt like a shadow. How would I survive four years?

John walked over and picked it up. "Why don't I talk to him for a while?"

I listened hazily to one side of the conversation that followed. John's usually gentle voice grew steadily louder, until he said firmly, "Yes! She is her mother's daughter. She has her mother's determination. And right now, all that determination is bent on not being here!"

When John handed the phone back to me, my father said, "Look, you have access to all the allowance money we budgeted for this semester. If you want to use it to buy a plane ticket, I can't stop you." That night, I slept.

In a scene from one of my father's favorite movies, the 1939 *Wuthering Heights* starring Merle Oberon and Laurence Olivier, the heroine, Catherine, races across a wild rain-drenched moor screaming for her lost love, Heathcliff. The movie ends with the two of them walking together over that same moor, reunited in death. Whenever my father saw me after time apart, he would throw his arms wide and shout, "Catherine!" and I would reply, "Heathcliff!" and run to embrace him.

As I stepped off the plane in San Francisco, I wondered whether my father would meet me, and if he did, what he would say. Would he still be angry? Would he let me stay at home while I figured out what to do next? I looked anxiously at the faces of the people waiting at baggage claim, as I descended the long escalator. The moment my father spotted me, he opened his arms.

"Catherine!"

"Heathcliff!"

A few days after returning, I sat on Judy's couch and tried to figure out what had happened. I tried to recall my sense of certainty, of conviction that I must return. But back in California, I felt only stupid, embarrassed, and lost. The rosy glow Santa Rosa had held for me during my final years of high school, and which I'd carried in my memory as I traveled across the country, had vanished the moment I set foot back inside the city limits. Without school and without my friends, the landscape seemed empty, drained of color. I had failed to grab hold of life, and it had left me behind.

For the first time in the twelve years I'd been coming to see her, Judy used the word *depression*. It seemed to fit what I felt—the listlessness, the graying-out of the world, the bone-deep fatigue—but I couldn't understand why I was feeling it now. I hadn't become depressed when my mother died, or when Jamie left for college, or when my father remarried. My emotional responses to those events had been sharp, vivid, sometimes overwhelming, but I'd never felt this kind of dull horror at the prospect of facing the next day.

I floundered in those first weeks at home, struggling to find a sustainable routine. I avoided the people I knew, ashamed to explain why I was still in town. Judy was the only person I saw regularly, and every week I found myself talking to her about my mother. In the past, when I'd thought of my mother's illness, I'd always considered it from my own perspective; but in the weeks and months after coming home I began to obsess, for the first time, about what the experience of dying must have been like for *her*. The video Jamie and I had watched together had provided a tiny insight into her perspective, and I was suddenly hungry for more. I tried to put myself in her position. I tried to imagine facing death, and leaving two small children behind. Sitting on Judy's soft leather couch, I speculated aloud about what it must have been like for her to wake up each morning with that heavy knowledge. How lonely, I thought, to be dying, when everyone around you gets to live.

I broke up with Zach in October. I hated being away from him, but I was so ashamed about running away from Tufts that I couldn't visit him at Stanford. He didn't argue. He was making his own new discoveries, forging a new identity, and it must have been difficult to divide his focus between life at college and his high school girlfriend back home. Within a year, Zach would come out as gay, a revelation that initially surprised me, but ultimately fast-tracked our evolution from exes to lifelong friends. Letting go of Zach felt like cutting one more tether that bound me to normalcy. I had no classes, no job, no relationship, and most of my friends had moved away. I felt utterly adrift.

But I had a place to stay. My father and Shirlee let me have my old room. They didn't charge me rent, and they let me add whatever I wanted to the grocery list. I also knew that, had they kicked me out, I could have stayed with a dozen other relatives or family friends. I had a network of people willing and able to support me while I figured things out. Without that network, I don't know what would have happened next.

Six weeks after I came home, I reconnected with my high school drama teacher, who mentioned that his wife was directing *The*

Grapes of Wrath at the Playhouse downtown, and that there might be a spot for me in the ensemble. It would be unpaid, but at least it would get me out of the house each day. Rehearsals for *Grapes* were already well underway when I showed up at the theater one evening. It was a large cast, and I had grown up watching several of the older actors perform at the local theaters. As low as I felt, being inside a theater again, with its familiar lighting, sounds, and smells, stabilized something within me. I'd never read the book by John Steinbeck, but as I watched Frank Galati's stage adaptation unfold before me over the next few weeks, the power of the script was undeniable. The production's set design included a river (a sunken trough filled with real water) running the width of the stage, in which the actors could fully submerge themselves. The effect when one of the leads cannonballed into the water, misting the first row of the audience in spray, was wonderful.

I had no lines, but I was onstage through most of the show. I'd be sitting by a tent or a campfire while other actors played a scene in the foreground, or I'd be square-dancing in a crowd scene or looking pathetic by the side of a dusty road. I learned how much specificity, how much life, I could bring to a character without pulling focus from the story. During one rehearsal, the director handed me a plastic baby doll wrapped in a blanket and said, "I want you to hold this doll and make the sound of a baby crying, but I don't want to be able to see your face move, okay?"

"Okay," I said, with no idea how to do what she was asking.

I spent that night practicing in my bedroom, until I could make a sound that, if it wasn't exactly a baby crying, might pass for a cat being strangled in the far distance. I stared into the mirror and made sure my face didn't move at all. This ability, which I dubbed "baby ventriloquism," came in handy in many subsequent plays, and remains on the special-skills section of my résumé to this day.

Once *Grapes* closed, I again had nothing to do. I began looking for part-time jobs (office work, retail), but the hours I'd spent in that theater watching a show come to life had been the only ones, since coming home from Boston, when I hadn't felt like a total failure. I made a list of all the theaters within a thirty-minute drive, and looked up all the upcoming auditions. It was already late fall, so the next thing in the pipeline was the annual production of *A Christmas Carol* at a theater in Sebastopol. I auditioned.

Rehearsals for *Carol* took place in the evenings, because all the other actors had day jobs. I needed something to fill the eight hours between waking up and driving to the theater, and I also needed a job that would pay me more than the $300 stipend I could expect at the end of the run. Through a lucky tip from a friend, I landed a gig playing Alice in a two-person stage adaptation of *Alice in Wonderland* that toured local elementary schools. The little show rehearsed and performed during the day, and I made $100 per show. Since my father allowed me to live at home rent-free, a few *Alice* shows per week were plenty to cover my minimal expenses.

That Christmas season Shirlee agreed to open our house to the Junior League, for their annual tour of historic homes. Our house was only thirty years old, but it was in a historic neighborhood, and that, it seemed, was enough. She decorated the place with evergreen boughs and holly and nutcrackers and stacks of silver gift boxes. I lay in bed, listening to footsteps make their way through the rooms. A little sign hung from my doorknob indicating the visitors should not enter. I felt like a plague sufferer, someone unfit to go out into normal society. Through my bedroom door, I heard Shirlee's son, David, speaking to someone. The voice sounded familiar. I inched my door open and peeked through. He was standing in the hall talking to a family friend. David was still living at home while attending the local junior college, something I wished I'd thought to try myself. The friend asked after me.

"How's Gwenny liking Tufts?"

"She dropped out," David said.

"Oh?" Her eyebrows went up with concern.

"Yeah," he said, "and Jamie got his girlfriend pregnant."

I closed the door. *True enough,* I thought. Then I imagined the look on my mother's face after hearing David's summary of our lives.

Jamie's twins were born a few days before Christmas. I wanted to visit right away, but my father asked me to wait a few weeks and let him visit first with Shirlee.

"Too many people might be overwhelming," he said. Then, "When the three of us are together, it makes Shirlee feel left out. You and Jamie are so close, it can be a bit intimidating."

I stared silently back at him, hoping he would hear the words coming out of his mouth and decide to take them back. He didn't, so I stayed behind.

They were fraternal twins, easily told apart, even in their earliest days of life. In their first photograph together, one baby's eyes are wide open, staring at its sleeping sibling as if to say, *So that's what you look like.*

I slept on the couch in their tiny rented house and tried to be helpful.

"It's good to have an extra person around," Jamie said. "We've learned there's really supposed to be one more grown-up than baby. You bring the numbers back in our favor."

I loved feeling that I had a place in their family. Looking at the four of them, two parents and two children, I felt I was regaining something long-lost.

After the holidays, I was cast in a production of David Mamet's *Oleanna*, and then *On the Road*, and then *A Midsummer Night's Dream*. All together I did eight plays that year. My father came to all of them, just as he had when I was in high school. He always brought me flowers and said I was wonderful. During that year, I learned how to audition; I learned rehearsal etiquette, performance etiquette, and the rhythm of an actor's days. That I was able to spend an entire year doing nothing but nonunion acting work is a testament to the enormous privilege of my circumstances. I never made much money, but each dollar felt like a tiny vote of confidence in my future. The first time I got a check in the mail for money I'd earned acting, I had to fight the impulse to frame it.

One day in late spring, I went up into the attic to look through the boxes of my mother's things. I wasn't looking for anything in particular; I only wanted to be surrounded by the things she had touched. The attic was a warm, dusty cave lined with silvery tubes of insulation. I peeked into the big wardrobe boxes holding the few pieces of her clothing we hadn't thrown away or donated. I ran my hands over the little knickknacks that used to sit on top of the low white bookcases lining her bedroom. Then, lifting the lid from a box of old papers, I glimpsed a gray audio-cassette in a plastic case. It looked just like the one on which my mother had recorded the letter for my first period, but this one had written on its edge: *Jamie and Gwenny*. I stared at it. What was it doing up in the attic? Was it from my mother? Or was it simply an old tape, used to record music? I thudded down the attic's wooden ladder and into my bedroom, where I opened the tape deck of my silver boom box. After a few moments of static, I heard a familiar voice.

July 1996

Dear Jamie and Gwenny,

How can it be possible that I am leaving you? It is unbearable, unthinkable, and yet, I must think of it. I can hardly think of anything else. You fill my heart and mind every moment. How can it be that you will grow up without me? Every day I beg God to let me live and stay with you.

In the time that is left to me, while I can still be up and about, I am preparing a keepsake box for each of you, filled with letters and gifts to mark many of the traditional milestones that await you. Of course, there will be special milestones, unique to each of you, which I cannot guess at now. But at least I can think about, and plan, for the traditional ones. Things like when you become a teenager, when you get your driver's license, when you graduate from high school, announce your engagement, marry, have your first child—all moments I so long to share with you.

Fashions change, and you and your interests will change, in ways I cannot anticipate. So I hope you will be able to feel the deep love and connection with which I prepare these tokens, even if they aren't quite what you might've chosen for yourselves. I am trying to be with you in spirit in an unknown future. Just know that I love you both with all of my heart and mind and being.

And please remember, although these mementos are precious because of their associations, they are still only things. They are only meant to serve as reminders of the great love I hold for you, and to help you maintain your sense of connection to your personal histories. Some are bound to get lost or broken or mislaid. Please try not to worry about it too much. Losing something I've given you is not the same as losing your connection to me. I am a part of your very selves. That can never be lost. Try not to be too hard on yourselves. I would say, that has been one of my greatest obstacles to happiness, I've been so hard on myself.

You may have very strong expectations about how you are supposed to feel or behave when I am gone, and judge yourselves harshly if you do not fulfill those expectations. Just go on being your bright, wonderful, joyful, funny, loving selves. Whatever you feel will be just what you are feeling, and will be appropriate for you in that moment. You are bound to have lots of different feelings, and they may be different from each other's, and different from Daddy's. You most likely will not get to "once and for all" in your feelings about my dying. Your feelings will go on changing with time, as you change and your lives change. Trust and love yourselves.

The voice on the tape began to break apart with emotion. Curling my body up to the silver speakers, I listened to my mother steady her voice.

I am crying as I write this, sitting at the dining room table. You are in the pool house, attending the second summer session of the Pocket School. In so many ways it all feels so normal, and yet I feel the moments passing, never to be recaptured, my time with you slipping away from me. Why can't I be wiser? How is it that I can allow myself to drift through a day with you, even now, knowing my time with you is short? Why have I not learned how to seize the essence of each day, suck the marrow from its depths, and offer it up to you as an irreplaceable gift? I don't seem to have the wisdom, the substance, the soulfulness to do this for us. I only know to hang on for dear life. Holding you close, telling you every minute how much I love you, how dear you are to me, how much I want to be with you.

But I can't spend every waking moment clinging to you. I must let you go to get on with your lives, growing, learning, preparing, and just experiencing what you can. I simply want to be at your sides helping you and loving you, it seems such small ambition, one every parent is entitled to. Why must it be beyond my reach?

I never really understood what the expression "life is for the living" meant until now. When you know yourself to be among the living, and think of your death as something that might happen in a distant future, if you think about it at all, then all seems possible, and one can be lavish with expenditures of time, with little thought as to content. When you know yourself to be among the dying, it is so difficult to remain in the fray, the great rush of movement and activity you take for being alive in the world. It all seems so pointless and futile, all the striving and activity and accumulations make no impression on death. But we are not taught how to make each moment count. Our culture and economy tell us the way to make the moments count is to fill up each one with activity and consumption. And if we can set ourselves apart from the pack through some sort of self-aggrandizing competence, so much the better. But death cannot be held at bay by wealth, or talent, or worldly power, or even by being good.

So what really matters at the end? Being true to ourselves and each other. Loving and being loved. Kindness and compassion. Being remembered with pleasure. Leaving the least amount of harm and pain and suffering behind us that we can. What about our works, our accomplishments? I don't know. I haven't anything of importance to leave behind me of my own making. You two are the only true treasures I leave behind, and you are of your own making.

We are given such a brief amount of time for the lessons of this life to transform us, transmute the lead of our material lives and perceptions into the gold of our spiritual selves. Somehow I must trust that I have been given enough time. Even though it hardly seems possible. Perhaps I have been given the time, and just did not know how to make the best use of it.

You two have taught me everything I know about love. You have been wonderful teachers. Just being your own true, wonderful selves has taught me how to love you with all of my being. You deserve to be loved and cherished and seen and heard and known and nurtured by me and Daddy and everyone else invited into your lives.

I love you,

Your Mommy

Just as I had when I was twelve, I lay on my bedroom floor and cried into the sound of static. The room around me had changed over the past six years. The rug beneath me was the color of oatmeal, and sometime in high school I'd painted my walls a deep terra-cotta red. The shrine Sobonfu had helped me build was gone. A black graduation cap sat jauntily on one side of my mirror.

In the years since losing my mother, I had dutifully opened the chest's contents, one by one, at the proper times. I had admired the gifts, and read the cards and letters, and tried to keep them all organized and safe. I had followed all my mother's instructions, but I had only been a passive participant in our conversation. I had accepted her gifts, her words, without much thought about the broader intention behind them. But now, as I rewound the tape and prepared to listen again, something new began to come into focus.

My mother had wanted to comfort us with the chests, to help us weather her loss. But she had also wanted to do something else.

In the recording, she had explicitly said that the objects inside the packages were not really the point, and even to forgive ourselves for losing them (I thought of the coral necklace, and felt an old knot loosen in my stomach). So what was the point?

I am trying to be with you in spirit in an unknown future.

My mother had known that our lives, any lives, would contain great challenges, and she had bitterly mourned the fact that she would not be there to help us face them. She had tried to put herself, her essence, into a container we could carry with us, so that when, like Vasilisa in the fairy tale, we found ourselves outmatched, we would have something, someone, to turn to. The person I needed to call upon for help in unsnarling the tangle of my life was not the smiling, gentle mother wrapping birthday gifts. The woman I needed was the woman from the tape, the woman from the videos, the person who had fought and suffered and lived a whole life before I existed. I needed all of my mother, not only the softest pieces of herself that she had shown me when I was small. She had left a trail of breadcrumbs to lead me toward my future, toward her, but in order to find them all, I would need to look much more closely. I would need to ask questions.

During my next session with Judy, I told her about the tape, and Judy reminded me that my mother too had seen a therapist for many years. I stared at her.

"Do you think she would talk to me?"

"Why don't I give her a call?" Judy said slowly. "A patient's death doesn't revoke confidentiality, but maybe she could speak with me, in general terms."

A week later, I ran up the steps to Judy's office, eager to hear what the therapist had said.

"So?" I asked, sitting on the sofa.

"It was the strangest thing," Judy said. "She almost seemed to be expecting my call. Right away she said, 'Oh yes, Kristina said that if either of her children ever came looking for information about her, I should tell them anything they wanted to know.'"

Dr. Bell's office looked a lot like Judy's, simple modern furniture, tasteful abstract prints, but Dr. Bell did not treat children, so there was no playroom and no sandbox. My palms tingled as I sat down in one of the two deep armchairs.

"So," she said, smiling at me as though we'd met many times before, "how can I help?"

I looked back at her. I had so many questions, and I couldn't put a single one into words.

"Would you like to know why your mother started seeing me?" she suggested.

"Yes."

"She was unhappy in her marriage."

It gave me a pang, even though I knew it already. She said it with such authority.

"When did she start seeing you?" I asked.

She named the year, glancing down at a folder in her lap.

Before I was born, I thought, which led me to the inevitable question: *Then why was I born?* I thought about my mother telling me that she'd been born to save her parents' marriage, and failed.

"Why was she unhappy?" I asked.

"Your mother was a very powerful personality. I think she married your father because she thought he'd be a good parent. He was playful and affectionate, and rather childlike himself. But those very qualities that she valued in him as a father, frustrated her in him as a husband. She felt she always had to be the grown-up."

I nodded; all of this made sense to me.

"She wanted an equal. I think she pushed and pushed your father, hoping to goad him into standing up to her. Instead, he retreated further and further away. He became accommodating and submissive, and then resented it.

"She was also working through her anger over her cancer diagnosis. She was furious that this was happening to her, to your family. It wasn't part of the plan."

I nodded again. My mother cared a lot about plans. I thought of the little menu cards listing our options for breakfast and lunch.

We talked for another few minutes before I found the courage, and the words, to ask the question I most wanted answered.

"Do you think my parents would have divorced, if my mother hadn't gotten sick?"

"Yes," said Dr. Bell without hesitation.

I took this in. "How can you be so sure?"

"Because they did divorce."

The room seemed to tilt very slightly. I wedged my elbows against the upholstered arms of the chair. Dr. Bell flipped through some of the pages in her file.

"Your parents had been struggling for a long time. They were running a business together, raising children together, and managing your mother's illness, all while trying to maintain their marriage. Then your mother joined a spiritual group. I think it was called the Village.

"My understanding is that through conversations with the leaders of this group, your mother decided that she and your father would be better at managing all the other aspects of their lives, a better team, if they stopped trying to be husband and wife. In other words, they would let that piece, the romantic piece, of the relationship go. I'm not sure how your father felt about this, but I know he agreed to it.

"They went through a ritual to release each other from their marriage vows. Partly because of your mother's illness, they hadn't had a physical relationship in a long time. I know she gave your father her blessing to seek that elsewhere, as long as it didn't affect your family, but, as far as she knew, he never took her up on it."

Questions jockeyed for position in my brain. The outlines of the room seemed strangely blurred, while certain details stood out too vividly—the plush pile of the carpet, the gold tip of the doctor's pen.

"When did they do this?"

"Sometime between 1997 and 1999," she said, scanning her notes, "on some property your mother's family owned near Mendocino."

Images blossomed in my brain: golden hayfields, redwood trees, morning mist clinging to the edges of a valley. We'd spent summers there when Jamie and I were little, staying in a ranch-style house with one fireplace, no insulation, and a gorgeous view of cows grazing in a meadow. My mother's grandparents had bought the land in the twenties and thirties, and it still belonged to our extended family. It was the place where Tippy had been born, a former sheep and cattle ranch. Mentally I walked the narrow dirt path, lined with ferns, into the dense bit of forest called the Cathedral Grove, where thousand-year-old trees towered hundreds of feet high. Some of the trunks had been hollowed out by fire, leaving holes wide enough to drive a truck through. Several of my cousins had gotten married in that grove. I wondered which spot my parents had chosen to enact their divorce.

"Did people know?"

"A few people, close friends. But I think it was mostly just for them: a fresh start, different priorities."

I remembered my mother calling me into her bedroom one

afternoon, soon after they'd sold the juice company. My father was sitting on the edge of her hospital bed, his arms around her.

"What is it?" I'd asked from the doorway.

"We just wanted you to see us like this," he said, laying his cheek against the top of my mother's head. They leaned close toward each other as though posing for a photograph. Obediently I clicked the shutter in my mind, freezing them like that.

I remembered other moments of gentleness between them in those final years. And, for the first time, I thought about how long my father had gone without a real relationship.

"You said she gave him permission . . . but he never took her up on it?"

"That's my understanding."

When my father began dating again, his marriage hadn't been over for months, it had been over for years. My grief at losing my mother had begun the day she died, but his grief was old by then, more scar than wound. I felt a weighty tug of sadness and love for my father. Why had he never told me this? And if my mother wanted me to know, why hadn't she told me herself? Or, if she'd felt I was too young, why hadn't she told Dr. Bell to contact me at a certain time? But as soon as the questions formed in my mind, the answer was there too: I had to want this information. I had to be the one to ask.

Walking down the steps away from her office door, I felt new spaces expanding in the oldest corners of my memory. I had learned to grip so tightly on to my own understanding of the past, terrified that time and change would wrest it from me. But what if the past was not as knowable as it had always seemed? What, exactly, was I holding on to?

I didn't immediately tell Jamie about what I'd learned in that quiet, tastefully decorated office. As a new father himself, I figured he had enough going on. I didn't discuss it with my father either.

The new understanding and affection I felt for him was too fresh and fragile to test against the hard rigors of conversation. I knew one of us was bound to say something that would tarnish the tender image I now held of our family, doing its best in an impossible situation. I didn't want to know whether he'd ever accepted my mother's offer of companionship elsewhere; I was too taken with the version of him that held fast to our family, even as we were sinking.

Although I had technically deferred from Tufts, I knew I would never go back. In the winter of my gap year, I applied to the University of California as a drama major, and by spring I had a spot at UC Berkeley. The campus was an hour from my house with no traffic. I'd felt a new sense of resilience in the months following my talk with Dr. Bell, but as the start of the fall semester approached, I felt all the old anxiety rise within me. By September, I was only slightly less terrified than I'd been to go to Boston.

My father helped me move into a triple dorm room in Stern Hall, a building nicknamed the Nunnery because it was all women. I remember almost nothing about the two pleasant young people whose room I shared. I was in such a daze of nausea and fear that I hardly spoke to them. All I wanted to do was sleep. I slept through every orientation, every get-to-know-you breakfast, every mixer where the women from Stern Hall got together with the men from Bowles, the dorm on the other side of the Greek Theatre. I woke up once a day to go to the dining hall, where I took things that were portable—a carton of milk, a wrapped sandwich—and carried them back to my bed to eat alone. Being alone was awful, but being around other people was worse. Among all those unfamiliar faces, I kept thinking I saw my five missing friends. The Sensational Six had gathered again at the beach house over the summer, and once again I'd written out a narrative of the weekend, and added it to the pasta sauce jar. My heart broke all over again when we scattered for school in the fall.

Classes, once they began, were the only thing that held me together. Something in my brain's hardwiring wouldn't allow me to sleep through the little time slots marked on my course schedule. I would rise from my extra-long twin like something between zombie and automaton, and march down the hill to attend lectures. When the lectures were over, I would gather up my notes, walk back up the hill, and get back into bed.

During those first grim weeks, a friend of my mother's who lived in nearby Mill Valley invited me out to dinner, and we met halfway at a bistro in Richmond. I drove my Volvo to the last exit before the bridge. At first my father had refused to allow me to bring the car with me to campus, fearing I would use it to come home. I'd told him that without the car, I didn't think I could go at all.

Anne and I sat across from each other in the dimly lighted restaurant, a huge burger in a shiny brioche bun in front of me. I couldn't bring myself to take a bite.

"Oh, my sweet," she said. She had always called me that. That was my name when we played hopscotch together in my driveway, tossing a stone or a dried seed casing across the numbered squares, jumping between the chalk lines. When she spent the night with my mother, she would let me brush and style her short red hair in the morning when she woke up. She called it "Gwenny's Salon."

Her sympathy undid me completely. So many people loved me and wanted to help, yet I couldn't see any way through the darkness. I couldn't imagine a future for myself. All I wanted was to go back to being the girl playing hopscotch, the girl with the pretend salon. (When I reminded Anne of that evening, years later, she nodded solemnly. "The saddest burger in the world," she said.)

A few days later, I called Jamie from a sunny bench on Berkeley's Sproul Plaza. It was a ridiculously beautiful day, and the tanned coeds all around me were drinking it in. I imagined a cartoon thundercloud over my own head.

"Why can't I do this?" I asked my brother, thousands of miles away. "Why is it so hard?"

"I don't know."

In the background, I could hear the babies crying. I felt pathetic. Jamie had real challenges to tackle, while mine were entirely self-created. What was wrong with me? I had a place at a great school and my whole future ahead. Why did I feel crammed into a tiny dark box? What would it take for me to stop clinging to a version of my home and family that had long since disintegrated? I wanted to fall asleep on that bench, and not wake up until after graduation.

"Maybe," Jamie said on the phone, sounding as though he was turning over a brand-new thought in his mind, "maybe college doesn't have to be a trial by fire. I don't think it's supposed to be this hard."

A few weeks into my first semester at Berkeley I packed up my books, my shower caddy, and my extra-long twin sheets, and loaded them into my car. I lied to my two roommates, telling them there was a family emergency. Then I drove home.

The first time I failed to leave home for college, my father was angry; the second time, he seemed scared. I told him I would commute to campus and keep attending all my classes.

"You can't isolate yourself this way," he said, "it's not good for you."

"I know," I said, "but I don't know what else to do."

I had no energy to argue, but I also knew I wasn't going back to my dorm. I had run up against some internal limit. It seemed the emotional tethers that kept me confined to my house in childhood had not vanished, but simply lengthened, and now I had exhausted all their slack.

That semester I racked up hundreds, then thousands of miles in my car. I came to know the stretch of roads and highways that connected my house to the parking garage on University Avenue, where I paid for a monthly pass, like a movement in a musical score. It could be sped up or slowed down, but the notes were always the same, and I knew every one of them by heart.

On campus I felt like an impostor, some strange half-beast, a chimera, neither fully a college student nor truly anything else. I did not want to make friends. I felt any offer of intimacy would destabilize me, tearing off the paper clips and rubber bands that were the only things holding me in the shape of a functioning person.

My father and I had the bitterest arguments of my life during the months I commuted to school. We fought more often and more intensely than when he'd begun seeing Shirlee. I'd never seen him so angry with me. He hated how much time I spent in bed. He again threatened to take away my car so I'd have to stay at school. I told him that if he did that, I'd stay home and find a job. I genuinely believed that without the comfort of returning to the house, I wouldn't be able to survive. I thought I might actually die of homesickness.

I still do the drive from Santa Rosa to Berkeley and back in my dreams. The long, uninterrupted stretch of highway to Marin, the swerve onto the Richmond Bridge, so hideous in one direction, so beautiful in the other. The sun on the water of the bay. The dingy storefronts along University Avenue, and the huge echoing garage where I'd leave my car for the twenty-minute walk to campus. From blocks away, you could smell the invasive eucalyptus that grew in great swaths along Strawberry Creek. The time I spent on campus was barely more than the time it took to get there and back. After pulling into our driveway, I'd go up to my room, get into bed, and fall asleep while it was still light.

That winter, at Judy's suggestion, I went to see a psychiatrist. Dr. Collins had pale-blond hair and wire-rimmed glasses. He had a pleasant face, and a certain quiet charisma. I gave him the Cliffs Notes of my life: my mother's illness and death, my inability to leave home, the way the advent of college had turned this lifelong quirk into a serious impediment.

"What do you wish would happen?" he asked. "If you close your eyes and imagine a solution to the problem, what does it look like?"

I tried.

"I wish college was already over. I wish I could skip to the other side of the next four years. Then I could come back to Santa Rosa, rent an apartment, get a job, and just move forward with the rest of my life without ever having to go away."

"Interesting," he said.

"Why?"

"Because in certain ways you seem both much older and much younger than your actual age. That wish you just described is a child's wish. You're wishing for magic, time travel."

This stung me a little.

"What would a grown-up wish for?"

"A grown-up would wish for the capacity to overcome the obstacle. A mature person doesn't seek to change the circumstances, but rather their own response to them."

I thought about this. I tried to wish that I could go to college, but couldn't manage it. All I wanted was to stay home, for everything to go back to the way it had been.

"I'm going to prescribe a very low dosage of antidepressants. It will take a few weeks to know if they're having any effect. Then we'll go from there. By the way," he asked as I stood up and gathered my things, "what are you studying?"

"Theater," I said, putting on my coat.

"What?" he asked sharply. "You're an actor?"

"Yeah," I said, puzzled, "why?"

"We've been talking for an hour and you didn't think to mention it?"

"What's the difference?"

"This whole session I've been talking to a performer. Now I have to reassess everything."

I left, not sure whether he was joking. I wondered if he was confusing the art of acting with the art of lying. Or maybe he would just write me off as a person enamored of her own drama.

The first antidepressant he prescribed kept me awake at night. The second made me sleep all day. But the third was like Goldilocks finding the perfect bowl of porridge. Ten milligrams a day, and I felt the floor reappear beneath my feet.

The medicine didn't solve everything. I still sometimes spent whole days in bed watching DVDs of *The West Wing*, but the change to my neurochemistry gave me a foundation to build on. The events of my life had made me comfortable accepting magic, and this was the closest thing to real magic I'd ever experienced. By winter break, I felt ready to try moving back to Berkeley. It couldn't be this simple, but it also could.

My father helped me find a room in a house off campus with five other women, a mix of students and young professionals. It was less expensive than the dorms, and I had my own room where I could retreat when I felt overwhelmed. The room came with a frame for a double bed, a luxury I'd never had before. My father tied Jamie's old double mattress to the top of his Toyota Highlander, like one of his huge Christmas trees, and drove it down to Berkeley for me. Then, because Jamie's mattress was firmer than what I was used to, he bought a large roll of memory foam and cut it down to size with an electric carving knife he bought for the purpose. I watched as he knelt on the floor with the buzzing blade, sawing away at the foam, and felt an overwhelming affection for him. He wanted so much to make things better, safer, more comfortable for me. He took me furniture shopping at People's Bazaar and bought me a little leather armchair to read in.

After he left, I looked around at my new room. The walls were painted a soft, cloudy gray. For the first time, I felt I'd found somewhere I could stay for a while. Like Jamie, I hadn't brought the cardboard chest with me to college. I worried something might happen to it, and removing it from my childhood bedroom would have felt too much like an admission that I no longer truly lived there. I liked to picture it, safely tucked into my closet, waiting for me to come back. During my years in Berkeley, I would retrieve each birthday gift a few days or weeks ahead of time. The day I officially moved into the off-campus housing, I pulled the package marked *College Graduation* from the chest and held it in my hands. For the last eighteen months, or the last nineteen years, I'd believed I would never open it. Now I placed it in my suitcase. Something to strive for; a gesture of hope.

When I came home for the winter holidays my junior year of college, I noticed the change in my father immediately. He seemed less aware of his physical surroundings, bumping into furniture, losing his footing. There was a strange, ethereal quality to the way he looked at me, as if one of us wasn't entirely there.

He was upset about work, he said. The private Catholic high school where he'd acted as CFO for many years had been suffering from diminishing enrollment. Though he oversaw the school's finances, he had no control over how many parents wanted to send their children to parochial school. Nevertheless, when the news came that the school would have to close at the end of the academic year, he took it as a personal failure.

Early in the vacation, my father and Shirlee sat me down at a restaurant that served both homemade scones and Mexican food, to explain that he'd been having a hard time getting out of bed in the morning. He'd been attending therapy and, like me, taking medication for anxiety and depression. To me, the school's closure seemed totally insufficient to explain the state in which I found him. It hadn't been his fault, and he had the financial stability to weather the loss of the job while he looked for another. He owned our home outright and had savings, and Shirlee earned a good income. I felt I was missing some crucial piece of the puzzle, but I didn't press him about it.

"Thank you for telling me," I said instead, after he'd finished. "You know, when Mommy was sick, I was still too young to be very helpful to her. If you'll let me, it would mean a lot if I could be helpful to you." I chose my words carefully. I didn't want to sound patronizing. I remembered the bleakness of my own depression, the way I'd felt worthless, like a waste of food and oxygen. I remembered, too, how angry he'd been with me during those months, and for the first time it occurred to me that his anger might have something to do with recognition.

"Thank you," he said, a mist gathering in the corners of his blue eyes. "In that case, I think we have a lot to talk about."

"You've been a good dad, you know," I said, hearing the triteness of the words even as they left my lips.

"Benign neglect, right?" He smiled. It was an old joke between us about his parenting style.

"Right," I said, smiling back.

During the winter recess, my father continued to go to work at the school five days a week, like the stalwart first mate of a foundering vessel. I had spent my teenage summers working in the school administrative offices, copying and filing and stuffing envelopes to earn some extra cash. I knew the kind, capable people who worked there, nearly all women, by name and coffee preference. My holiday break lasted nearly a month, and during that time, my father asked me to go in to work with him and resume my temp work to lend him "moral support."

Monday through Friday, in the weeks leading up to Christmas, I went into the office and did a little filing, or relieved the receptionist at the front desk, answering the phones while playing solitaire on her desktop. Occasionally I would poke my head into the room where my father typed away, hunt-and-peck style, at the standing desk he'd bought when his back began to bother him, and ask him about the proper home for a stray document, or bring him something to sign.

"Thank you," he said each time, his eyes filling as if I'd brought him a wrapped gift. "You're wonderful."

Around 2 p.m. we'd go for a late lunch at a nearby diner, where he ordered the French onion soup and I had a turkey sandwich. It reminded me of the Thursday evenings we'd spent meeting his old girlfriend for dinner, except it was my fantasy version, where it was just the two of us. After the server set down our meal, my father would spoon up a mouthful of his soup's gooey, toasted crust, and begin to talk about the past.

He spoke about his childhood in Yemen and Singapore, where his father had worked as a civil engineer, and later in England, where he was sent to boarding school when he was seven. During our childhoods, the stories my father told Jamie and me about boarding school only captured the mischief and magic of the place: raiding the kitchen for late-night feasts, coordinated attacks on other dormitories where unsuspecting, dreaming boys would be beaten senseless with pillows, or flipped bodily beneath their mattresses. But now he spoke of the loneliness, of missing his parents, of never being allowed to cry.

He spoke about leaving London for San Francisco in his twenties, and about meeting my mother. He reminisced about their early years buying and running Mrs. Wiggles Rocket Juice, and our life as a family when Jamie and I were small, before anyone got sick. A glossy sheen lay over the events as he recounted them, as if he'd forgotten all the late-night arguments that emanated through the walls in our house, as if we'd all passed together through a golden age.

I sat and listened and tried to be comforting. It seemed that something, a lock, a dam, had given way inside him, and from the broken barrier gushed a river of recollections, of words. I had wanted these words, craved them for years, dreamed that one day my father would acknowledge that, yes, we had lived a whole life together before everything changed, and parts of it were beautiful. But the words, when they came, did not organize themselves by theme or chronology, or by any other logic I could discern. He interrupted himself, repeated himself, lost the thread. The flood of anecdotes had no linear flow; rather, it spiraled into narrowing circles, a whirlpool with something dark and empty at its center.

On the weekends, my father, an early riser all my life, stayed in bed until noon watching the entire box set of Peter Jackson's *Lord of the Rings* adaptations. Through his door I could hear the sounds of battle as humans, elves, and dwarves stormed the bastions of evil, fighting demons they could see. I never thought of talking to Shirlee about what was going on. It would have been like admitting that, by now, she knew my father better than I did. On the last Sunday before Christmas, I rapped on my father's door around eleven and said it was time to get a Christmas tree. For two weeks I'd been suggesting we drive to the tree farm, but he'd demurred, saying we'd do it later.

Once we were there, he seemed to stand up straighter in the cold, bright air, saw in hand, tape measure in his pocket. During the depths of my own depression, familiar activities, even the ones I resisted, had always made me feel a little better. We felled another towering pine and lashed it to the roof of the car. On the way home, my father played the King's College Choir on CD, and even sang along to his favorite carol, "Once in Royal David's City." But at home, he left the tree propped in the driveway and went back to his room. In past years he'd always seemed to set the enormous tree in place single-handed, in the time it took Jamie and me to wash the sap from our hands and boil water for hot chocolate. We would turn around and the thing would be done. But that year, the tree stayed in the driveway for three days, getting rained on.

"Well, I'm putting it up," I said on the fourth day. "But *someone* should probably help me, or I don't know what will happen." I could hear the infantilizing lilt in my voice. I didn't know how I should speak to my father, so I settled for the way my father used to speak to me. He laughed, and together we levered the thick, resinous column into place, its needles still sparkling with the wet from outside.

Jamie arrived with his family late on Christmas Eve, and that night my sister-in-law and I busied ourselves filling stockings for the twins, who had just turned three. We wrapped the candy and toys in white tissue paper because that was what my parents had always done. It was sweet and strange to find myself on the other side of this familiar tradition, making the illusion happen for someone else.

The presence of his grandchildren seemed to bolster my father's spirits. He carried them, one then the other, on his shoulders, or trailed behind them as they wobbled around the backyard. They were nearly as old as I had been when we first moved into the house. Grandfatherhood was what my father was designed for, I thought, all of the fun and none of the discipline. During this visit, Jamie and I did not knock on each other's doors to leaf through old photo albums. Instead, we stayed up late laughing and drinking wine with Sally, while their children slept above us in Jamie's childhood bedroom. I was twenty-one, and Jamie was twenty-five with two children, and I felt we were very, very grown-up.

I told Jamie and Sally about our father's long mornings in bed watching films. During their visit, when he became unusually forgetful or switched rapidly from cheerfulness to anger and back again, Jamie and I would raise our eyebrows at each other as if to say, *That was weird, right?* But we thought of it like a rough patch, like weather, something that would pass.

Jamie and his family left early in the new year, but I stayed nearly two more weeks. When my father went back to work, I went with him, and we fell into the same routine, typing and filing, followed by late lunches filled with meandering, disjointed monologues.

On my last night at home, we talked about his plans for after the school closed. He said he was thinking of starting a nonprofit. There was an organization in the UK whose sole purpose was to place collections of poetry in doctors' waiting rooms. The idea appealed to him in its simplicity, its humanity. He said he might start an American version.

"Maybe I'll travel a bit first," he said. "I'll certainly be visiting you more often in Berkeley."

"I'm in a play that opens in March," I said. "Come then."

The next afternoon, as I packed my car to return to school, my father's white Toyota screeched into the driveway. He'd forgotten something at home, and driven back from work to retrieve it. We hugged standing in the street. My British father always struggled to hug me the way I wanted to be hugged. He would fold me in his arms for a few seconds, then begin to let go while I held on, wanting more time to lay my head against his chest, breathing him in. He'd replace his arms around me for a moment, then withdraw them again. That day, I held him tightly through four or five rounds of this familiar dance. He hugged and released, hugged and released, until finally I'd had enough, and I let him go for the last time.

That morning, brushing my teeth, I'd found a note he'd left next to the bathroom sink. Ever since I'd learned to read, my father had left me notes on tables and counters. He slid them under my bedroom door early in the morning, and tucked them under the windshield wipers of my car. Frequently the notes contained instructions: *Empty the dishwasher; Let Tippy out. Be home by midnight.* As I got older and our schedules continued to diverge, these notes became his primary mode of communication, of parenting. Even when texting no longer cost ten cents per message, he preferred to write down his missives in black ballpoint on pieces of five-by-seven-inch cardstock with his first and last names printed at the top. *Love, Daddy* always appeared at the bottom of the card. He often wrote *Daddy* differently from the rest of the words. He didn't print the letters, but signed them, as though "Daddy" were his name.

Peter Kingston

Gwenny,
    I love you. Have a
bold return to Berkeley.
Looking Forward to seeing your
new play. Love Daddy

PART THREE

The thing I'd never thought to dread happened on a Tuesday afternoon. On the second day of the spring semester, my stepbrother's name lit up my phone. This was unusual, and I paused in the act of gathering my script, water bottle, keys. I was heading out the door to attend the first read-through of the play I was rehearsing with the college theater department, the one I'd told my father about. I pressed Ignore, but when the phone rang a second time, I answered.

"Hello?"

"Gwenny, something happened. It's the worst thing ever."

I thought he was going to say the house had burned down.

"What is it?"

"Peter hung himself."

Hanged, I thought but did not say. When I was eleven, I'd read E. L. Konigsburg's *The View from Saturday*, and learned that the past tense for hanging things—pictures, towels, ornaments—was *hung,* and the past tense for hanging people—fathers—was *hanged.* I'd liked knowing this bit of trivia; it made me feel erudite.

"Is this a joke?" I asked. My stomach felt as though my foot had missed a stair, but my brain still insisted that what David had said was not, could not be, true. "If it's a joke, it isn't funny."

"No, I swear!"

"Okay," I said. "Well, is he . . . ?" The word hovered just out of reach. I grasped for it: ". . . dead?"

"I think he is."

My mind clung to the doubt in his voice. "Are the police there?"

"Yeah."

"Then put them on the phone."

A brief pause; then a deeper, more authoritative voice spoke. "Hello?"

"Hello," I said, feeling as if I were speaking lines in a play, or a game of make-believe—*you be the police, I'll be the daughter.* "Are you the police?"

"Yes."

"David said that Peter Kingston is"—again the word eluded me—"dead. Is that true?"

"I'm afraid so."

Standing in my college bedroom, with its cloud-gray walls, its assembly of thrifted and borrowed furniture, its profusion of open books and unfolded clothes, I felt my knees go slack beneath me. I sat down hard on the little brown leather armchair my father had bought for me on the day I moved in. I hung up, sat still for a moment, then called David back.

"Hi, sorry, can I talk to the police again?"

The same deep voice spoke.

"It's me again, sorry. Just to be clear, you're *sure* that he's dead? You've, like, checked?"

"Yes."

"Okay. Sorry. Thanks."

I put down the phone.

Then an enormous sound came out of me, grinding and shrill. It seemed larger than I was, as if it were generating me, instead of the other way around. The sound echoed through the six-bedroom house, but it was late afternoon and no one else was home. I could scream and scream, and no one would hear, but instead I got quiet, and tried to think of a way out of this, a way to turn back time. If this had only just happened, there was still a chance to change it, but the more time that passed, the harder it would be. All my life I had failed to stop the forward rush of time, but now, sitting in the leather armchair, things did seem to slow, to suspend. It seemed to me that the bedroom had somehow filled with water, or thin mist, and shadowy objects were floating all around: exotic fish, or missed opportunities, or unsaid words. I felt myself thrust backward into a landscape both familiar and foreign, a city I'd once visited in a dream, or another life. The contents of the room swirled about me, all the books and shoes and photographs I'd arranged like amulets to ward off the looming homesickness, the fear of what would happen if I ever left the place where I belonged. But I had left, and it had happened.

A single thought emerged, whole, from the mist. At first, I saw it from a long way off, like a street sign whose words I couldn't yet read. *Jamie*, was the first piece to come into focus. Then: *I have to call Jamie.*

Immediately it was obvious. Jamie would not hear this news from David or the police, from someone who had loved our father less than he did. He would hear it from me. But something still slowed my dialing fingers as I lifted the phone from the arm of the chair. Jamie was still living in a world where our father was alive. *Let him stay in that world,* I thought, *for a few more seconds.*

His voice on the other end of the line was cheerful, normal. He sounded glad to hear from me. And all at once, I felt a huge, overwhelming doubt. There had been some mistake. Maybe I hadn't spoken to a real cop. Maybe I was hallucinating. How could I take responsibility for the truth of this information? I hadn't even seen a body.

I asked Jamie if Sally was with him. My own voice sounded oddly tentative, as though picking its way over sharp rocks.

"Yes," he said, "she's right here."

"So, I just talked to the police, and they're saying"—I tried to position myself as the purveyor of the information, rather than its source—"that Daddy—that he's dead."

"Oh," Jamie said. It was the same word he'd spoken when I told him we'd put Tippy down, but this time the syllable held shock, fear. "What happened?"

"They're saying," I said again, "that he killed himself. He hanged himself."

Three thousand miles away, I heard Jamie begin to cry. It had been ten years to the month since the night we walked into our mother's room to sit beside her body. Now, as then, Jamie, who rarely cried, wept freely, while I, a frequent crier, could not find my way to tears.

"I'm sorry," I said, "I'm so sorry."

"Yeah," he said, when he'd found his voice, "me too."

"I guess we should go home," I said, because that was still the name I gave to the house where we'd grown up.

"Yeah," he said, "I'll get a ticket. I'll be there as soon as I can."

"I love you," we said, and hung up.

Next I called Kim, the person who'd helped me with my college applications, and who'd been my father's closest friend for many years. I reached her at her office where she worked for our county's district attorney. At first she refused to believe me, saying I must have made a mistake. I understood how she felt. I hated insisting on this truth.

"Okay," she said finally, "I'll come get you. You shouldn't drive."

"You shouldn't either," I said.

"I'll be fine," she said firmly, and hung up.

Then I dialed the number listed on the contact page of my play script. I wouldn't be able to make it to the read-through that evening, I told the person who answered. Someone, I said, had died.

Lastly, I called Freesia in New York.

"I don't know what to do," I whispered. Whatever control I'd temporarily found was slipping, and my breath was a frantic animal.

"There's nothing to do," she said. "Just breathe."

"I'm scared," I said.

"Of what?"

I gulped air.

"I'm scared I won't be able to bear it."

They're just feelings, Judy had said to me for most of my life, *A feeling cannot kill you.* But at that moment, I worried she might have been wrong.

"Look at it this way," said Freesia, "in thirty years, when all the rest of our parents are dying, you'll already be done."

"That's . . ." I paused, stunned. "That's the least comforting thing you could possibly say."

"I know," she said sadly. "I thought maybe if I could make you laugh or make you mad, it might help."

It didn't help. In that moment, I felt certain that nothing would ever help.

Kim was at my door so quickly I knew she couldn't have obeyed the speed limits. She'd flown along the roads between Santa Rosa and Berkeley the way I did, the way my father would have.

I opened the front door to let her in.

"Your mother would be so pissed."

Later that night, when I returned to the house where I had once lived with my family, and where Shirlee now lived with her son, I saw my father's briefcase sitting on the table in the front hall. My father had carried the same briefcase for as long as I could remember. It was made of scarred and battered leather, the color of red clay, and fastened with a combination lock set to the date of my mother's and my shared birthday. All through my childhood, the briefcase's presence in the front hall signaled that my father was home, its absence that he was gone. Now it was there, but he was not. In the case he kept everything that needed his attention: business documents, car repair orders, overdue permission slips. If he had written a suicide note, I felt certain it would be inside.

The briefcase, like the cardboard chest, was held closed by two metal latches. Distantly, I felt something like surprise that my mother had not included a package labeled *Daddy's death* in the chest's table of contents. She seemed to have prepared for everything, everything except this. When I lined up the digits of our birthday and opened the briefcase, I found nothing out of the ordinary, no clue about what had been running through my father's mind on the last day of his life. He'd written me hundreds of messages in my life, but in those final moments, he'd chosen silence, the blank page. I thought of all the letters and packages still waiting inside the cardboard chest, and felt I would have traded them all for one brief, scribbled note.

That night, Kim took me home with her and put me in a hot bath.

"I want you here," Shirlee had said tearfully when I'd come by the house, along with so many other people, friends and family there to deliver food and sit in chairs. But I couldn't face my childhood bedroom. I couldn't face the colorful fabric bird my father had bought and hung from my ceiling, or the bank of windows he had opened each night during the summers to cool the air as I slept, and closed each morning before the fog burned from the sky. For years that room had been the only place in the world I felt completely safe, but now the spell had broken, and if I walked inside I would have to acknowledge that its magic, if it had ever existed, was gone. I ran the warm tap in Kim's tub until the water was as hot as I could stand, and red lines appeared, marking its levels on my skin. The gush from the faucet pounded the surface with a sound like a storm.

Afterward we sat on her couch watching *Body Heat* in our pajamas, because neither of us was ready to try for sleep. I remember almost nothing about the film, which I'd never seen before, except Kathleen Turner's long legs and deep voice, and the way she tossed her hair over one shoulder, then the other. Over the dialogue, my brain looped a repeating tape of every conversation I'd had with my father over the past month. I plucked out words and phrases, turning them over and over, searching for hidden meanings, for the clues I had missed. What had he been trying to tell me?

I thought of a day, years before, when I'd been xeroxing something in the office of the school where my father worked, and the receptionist had poked her head in to tell me my father was in the hospital.

"He's okay," she said, "but they want to keep him for a few more hours to run some tests, and he called to ask if you would bring him lunch."

I drove the two miles to the Kaiser Permanente medical center, wondering how my father, who I'd thought was still working just down the hall, had wound up in the hospital without me knowing. I hadn't heard an ambulance drive up.

I carried the turkey wrap I'd picked up at a nearby grocery store through the wide fluorescent-lit hallways, until I found my father in a small room, sitting on a paper-covered exam table. He grinned sheepishly as I walked in.

"What happened?"

"I was having some chest pains, so I drove myself over to get checked out."

"You thought you might be having a heart attack, and you decided to get in a car and drive?" I spluttered. "I was ten feet down the hall, why didn't you ask me to drive you?"

"I didn't want to worry you," he said. He'd waited until he was confident everything was fine before involving me at all. He tore open the paper printed with the logo of the grocery chain, and took an appreciative bite of turkey. "I thought you'd had enough of seeing your parents sick in hospitals."

My father, I remembered, sitting on Kim's couch, would never have let me know how bad things really were; his instinct was always to spare me what he could.

In the hospital, they'd put him on a treadmill for a stress test. Nothing, they'd said, was wrong with his heart.

In the morning, we went to view the body. I wished I could have seen it on the spot where he fell, but the police had taken it away before I ever arrived at the house. I was nervous to see how he would look; I did not know what strangulation did to a person. I did not, in fact, know whether he had been strangled or broken his neck, and I didn't know how to ask. I had to pause and lean against the doorway of the big empty room with the single table at its center, my breath coming in shallow sips. It was like wading into an icy lake.

"Come on," Shirlee said, grasping my hand and tugging me in after her.

She walked purposefully toward the table and leaned over the form lying still on its surface. I suddenly remembered that, for years, she had been a hospital chaplain, and that she had seen a lot of death.

My father's skin looked waxy and pale, not bloodshot, as I'd feared. A white sheet came up to his chin, hiding any marks left by the rope. His mouth looked set and stern, as it never had in life, his lips collapsing over his teeth. Someone had closed his eyes.

"It's still him," Shirlee said to me over her shoulder, "he's just cold." And, without hesitation, she bent down and kissed his mouth.

She loved him, I thought, hovering a few feet behind her, *she really loved him.*

For years, my father built ropes courses as a hobby. He'd been a Boy Scout and knew a great many different knots, some of which he taught Jamie and me to tie. He constructed his first course around a ring of oak trees on our mother's family ranch. He spent days up a ladder, only his Nike tennis shoes and tall white socks visible beneath the growth of leaves. He sank steel eyebolts deep into the sappy trunks, and strung long coils of nylon rope from tree to tree. The result was a spiderweb of bridges hanging ten feet off the ground and leading to a huge net, meant to hold shipping cargo, that dangled like an enormous hammock and was capable of holding five or six people at once. Down the middle of this tangle ran a small zipline on steel cables, connecting two wooden platforms anchored to the trees with long metal screws. In summer, Jamie and I, our cousins and friends, swarmed over his homemade playground like squirrels, shimmying from branch to branch, lying suspended in the latticed green light.

He built several more courses in subsequent years, one of them in our backyard. He wove together the oaks, the pines, and the huge redwood tree that stood in one corner of our property with a swaying network of sturdy white cords. Jamie shot an arrow, carrying one end of a bit of fishing line, over the highest branch of the tallest pine so our father could feed a length of rope over the limb, and use it to hoist a hanging canvas chair on a pulley system up over the leafy canopy. Sitting in the chair, you could see out over the rooftops of the neighborhood. Ropes and trees: these were things my father had loved. He knew how to tie a knot that would not loosen. He knew how to hoist a person into the air and keep them there, defying gravity.

Part of me was grateful my father hadn't gone to some anonymous hotel with a pocket full of pills, or thrown himself from a high bridge into cold water. Instead, he had gone to a place he loved. The last thing he would have seen was the garden he had tended, and the last things he would have heard were the wind chimes by the back door.

On the day he died, I'd asked David to describe finding my father's body. I needed to picture it. He said that, from a distance, he'd thought my father was simply standing among the trees. That in itself was odd. My father rarely stood still. He was always finding a fence to mend, a shrub to plant, or a tree to prune. David had called out to him but got no response. Then he moved closer, and realized my father's feet weren't touching the ground.

I picked Jamie up at the airport, as I'd done so many times before when he came home from college. He and Sally had come alone, leaving the twins with her parents. I put my arms around his neck, and the scratch of his stubble against my cheek felt wonderfully, horribly real. For the hundredth time I thought, *This is not a dream.*

We went back to the funeral home together, so that Jamie could see the body for himself. When I walked into the viewing room, I was startled to see that, in the two days since I'd last been there, someone had dressed my father's body in a suit and given him a full face of makeup. Thick foundation coated his skin, and his lips were painted pink.

"He—it wasn't like this before," I said lamely. I would have warned him. I'd never seen a dead body made-up. It seemed bizarre that a man who never wore makeup in life (except for the time he came to one of Jamie's birthday parties dressed as the Queen of Hearts) should be caked with it after death. I stood at his head, and Jamie stood at his feet.

"I think he looks less weird from upside down," I said. "Want to switch places?"

We switched. Jamie didn't feel it helped.

From my new position, I noticed a scuff mark on the sole of one shoe, then wondered why he needed shoes. Everything about the form on the table, the shoes, the suit, the makeup, seemed so very far away from the person I'd lost.

After my father's death, the story of my mother discovering him with his shotgun, all those years before when their company teetered on the brink of failure, slowly unearthed itself, too late, from the depths of my memory. At first I wondered if I'd invented it. I could not recall who had told me the story or when, but as I repeated it to aunts, uncles, friends, they all assured me it was true. *Oh,* I thought, a new facet of regret expanding within me, *so there was a warning after all.* Shirlee had also known the story, and had taken steps to remove my father's hunting rifles from the house months before. When I heard this, I could only feel astonished at my own failure to accurately assess the situation during my month at home. I knew my father was depressed. I knew about his brush with suicide fifteen years earlier when he'd felt like a professional failure. I knew about the closure of the school. Somehow, I had not connected these dots.

For years afterward, I would feel the need to pick apart my father's final weeks, to square his behavior with lists of suicidal indicators I found online, on sites that ranged from official to highly questionable. I considered the life my father had left behind, examining it like the hollow husk shed by a snake, noting the ways his world had narrowed in the preceding years. Jamie and I had left home. My mother's large, sprawling family had mostly fallen from his life since his remarriage; some bridges burned in fiery arguments, others disintegrated from lack of use. Only the Qs remained close to him and his new wife. His own small family lived in England: a father, sister, nieces and a nephew, whom he visited every year or two. He'd lost a best friend when the friend's wife ran against Shirlee for a position in local government. For more than a decade, he and Kim had run their dogs together in the mornings, but this had stopped during his months of deep depression. The school where he worked, and which would soon close, provided most of his social interactions each day.

For years I speculated with my therapist, and with Jamie, and with countless friends and family members, talking late into the night over cups of tea, or wine, about whether or not he had known a month, a week, a day before that he was nearing the end. I tried framing his death in terms of the task our mother's illness had implicitly set him: to live until their children were grown. Maybe he felt he'd done his duty by launching us into the world. Maybe it had nothing to do with us at all. Maybe he was simply tired of riding the waves of depression. Maybe he couldn't face pulling himself up from the depths one more time. But none of these analyses could yield the answer that felt satisfactory, the answer that brought him back. "Why?" was entirely the wrong question, and yet it was the one I couldn't stop asking.

For our last Christmas together, Jamie and I had given our father a long, soft, blue bathrobe. I'd gone shopping at a big department store where I'd asked a harried employee to point me toward the "dressing gowns."

"What are you looking for?" he asked, eyebrows scrunched together.

"A dressing gown." I mimed tying something around my waist. "You know, like you wear when you get out of the shower?"

"She wants a bathrobe," Freesia translated. She'd come along to do some shopping of her own. Immediately the shop assistant led the way.

I'd lived in the United States my entire life, but I still occasionally tripped over stray bits of vocabulary: *lift*, *lorry*, *jumper*. These breakdowns in communication always caught me off guard, each one a tiny reminder that I was raised by a man who was from somewhere else.

On Christmas morning, my father admired the robe, thanked us, and then lifted an oddly shaped package from the pile and handed it to me. I tore off the paper to reveal a metal butterfly the size of an open encyclopedia. The steel of its wings was oxidized into rainbows. Its antennae were long and flat, and trembled when touched. The tips of its hind wings were thin and sharp as tin can lids. I sat amidst the bright wreckage of Christmas morning, holding its considerable weight in my lap, utterly confused.

"Thank you," I said, looking into my father's hopeful face. I didn't know what else to say. The butterfly had two holes in its thorax for screwing to a deck railing or the trunk of a tree. I lived in one rented room, in a house with five other women, and had nowhere to mount the enormous metal insect. It was like something you might dangle over a child's crib so she could watch the light reflect off its rainbow wings, only much larger, heavier, and dangerous to touch.

"I saw it in the garden store," he said, "and it made me think of you."

My father loved the garden store. He loved puttering around our big backyard, and had his own extensive collection of decorative animals. Small stone rabbits peeked out between clumps of violets, a long carved serpent undulated in and out of the ground by the back gate, and a Mexican ceramic rooster presided over the redwood steps of the back deck. Was this meant to be the first piece in a collection of my own? Did it symbolize my adulthood, and readiness for a home with a garden? Had I, at some point, expressed a great love of butterflies?

I used to catch butterflies in my hands as a child of eight or nine. The grassy field of my elementary school was full of monarchs, painted ladies, and cabbage whites. I'd close two cupped palms over an insect and feel the flutter of its wings against my skin like a tiny motor. There would always be four or five other girls butterfly hunting, and when one of us caught something we'd announce it loudly, and hold our sealed hands out to the others. Everyone would gather around to stare at the backs of the lucky girl's fingers. She couldn't show us her butterfly, or it would escape. Sometimes I'd just pretend to catch one, so that I could hold the place at the center of the circle, with only air between my palms. When the bell signaled the end of recess we'd fling our catches back into the sky, before running across the field to take our places in line. I hadn't caught a butterfly in at least ten years.

"Thank you," I said again, and hugged him.

Back in Berkeley, I shoved the butterfly into the back of my closet, and forgot about it until a few days later, when I was looking for something to wear to the memorial. Its heavy metal body made a harsh *clang!* as I dragged it out. I held it by its two rigid wings like a binder full of script pages or choir music. I knew that I would not be able to throw it away now, this last thing my father had given me.

Nearly five hundred people attended the memorial. I turned a corner and saw a parking lot stuffed with cars, glinting in the late January sun. I stepped into the high-ceilinged lobby of the auditorium to find nearly everyone I'd ever known. If only, I thought, we could have gathered the week before my father died, instead of the week after. *Look,* the huge crowd would have told him, *look how valued you are, look how loved.*

The same long-haired, guitar-playing pastor who had married my father and Shirlee seven years earlier conducted his service. I remember none of his words, just my gratitude that he did not condemn or moralize, only lamented the magnitude of our loss. People spoke, and the words accumulated like grains of sand, filling some small corner of a vast hollow space. David stood up, unexpectedly, to say that he was sorry if he'd done anything to make my father want to die. For the first time, I wondered if anyone was ensuring that David, who'd been the one to find the body, had someone to talk to about it.

I sat beside Jamie in the front row, wearing my mother's pearls and the only black skirt I'd found in my closet, which had a small tear in the side seam showing a fingernail crescent of skin, folding and unfolding the page I'd printed before leaving the house.

That morning, Jamie and I had walked with Uncle Ward through the cemetery. We'd picked our way among the tangled paths until we found our mother's grave. The amaryllis bella-donna I'd planted was dormant and covered in a carpet of fallen leaves.

"Kids," Uncle Ward said, sitting on the low concrete wall across from the headstone, "you were dealt some really high cards and some really low cards in this life."

The morning was bright and cold, the graveyard dappled all over in deep green shadow. I kicked at the sharp leaves beneath my feet, thinking that over. Through the luck of the draw, Jamie and I had been born into lives of privilege, comfort, and protection. We'd spent our childhoods with parents who loved us and could pro-vide for us. Losing them changed none of that. It was a moot point whether we would have traded the material gifts of our lives for more time to talk, laugh, and cry with them. Of course we would. And of course we couldn't.

For days I'd been trying to get something on paper to read at the memorial, but nothing would stick to the page. During those days, I'd heard over and over that it was all right for me to feel angry about what my father had done. It reminded me of the lady with the embroidered pillows who came to visit from hospice when I was a child. Again the option of anger was laid before me, and again I had no idea what to do with it. I felt no anger toward my father, only a deep, protective, nearly frantic sadness. It was as though he and I had been walking together, and he'd suddenly turned to show me a fatal wound I had no idea he'd suffered. The extent of his despair, and my failure to recognize it, left me physically weak every time I thought about it. It was this despair that I located as the cause of his death, more than the noose or the hands that tied it. I saw the fact of his death as proof that his life had become unbearable to him. His decision to die was evidence enough, for me, that he felt he had no other choice.

I shoved my hands deeper in the pockets of my hoodie. There was a faint, pleasant, smoky smell to the air. Someone, somewhere, was burning dead leaves.

"I don't know what to say this afternoon," I said.

"Of course not," said Uncle Ward. "But if you did know what to say, what would it be?"

At the memorial reception, the Sensational Six piled together on a single sofa, our arms and legs interlocking.

"You look like a pile of puppies," one passerby observed.

We still got together at least once a year, and we'd retained the physical intimacy common to friendships formed in childhood, when bodily boundaries are still soft and pliable. I was grateful to lose myself in the tangle of limbs, one part of a many-legged animal. They had not asked whether I needed them. They had simply come.

Later that night, after a couple glasses of red wine, I went to find Jamie.

"If I'm ever dumb enough to get married," I asked tipsily, "will you give me away?"

It was a strange thing to say to someone who'd been married three years, but he just smiled.

"Of course," he said, putting a hand on my shoulder.

"Okay, good."

The question was an emotional reflex. I wanted reassurance that there were people in my life to fill the roles my father had left vacant. But at the same time, I couldn't bring myself to ask it simply, vulnerably. The whole enterprise of marriage seemed more and more cursed to me. Both my father's marriages had ended in someone's early death. The lesson, at that moment, seemed clear: *Make a family, and the world will find a way to break it.*

. . .

Later in the evening I would encounter the kind doctor who'd given my mother his place in the cemetery.

"Did I ever tell you," he would ask, "how your mother asked me for the plot?"

"No," I would say.

Even if he had, I would have asked him to tell me the story again. For ten years I'd lived on scraps of information about my mother, laying objects and letters and anecdotes together in the shape of the person I'd lost. I spent time with her friends because I loved them, but also because, at any moment, one of them might see something—a tree, a restaurant, a look on my face—that reminded them of her.

"Did I ever tell you . . . ?" they'd begin, and I'd have one more memory to add to my collection.

"Did I ever tell you" had become my five favorite words. They signaled that I was about to be transported, carried on the magic of someone else's words, into the past.

We buried my father in the new part of the cemetery, with its rolling green lawns and colorful plastic flowers. I'd assumed he would be cremated, like my mother, but Shirlee wanted a burial.

We stood around the little hole in the earth as the coffin was lowered. On the bottom of the grave, someone had poured a layer of cement. Strange, I thought, to place so many barriers between our dead and the earth. My father's body had been put in a box, and that box would go into a hole lined with concrete. I tried not to think about how long it would take for him to decompose.

There were about ten of us gathered at the gravesite. Uncle Q placed a little plastic frog—the kind that can squirt water from a hole in its mouth—onto the coffin's wooden lid, a final salute to his fellow lover of pranks and games. When it was my turn to pay my respects, I recited a few lines from Tennyson's "The Lady of Shalott." For as long as I could remember, my father had had a framed print of the painting by Waterhouse, depicting her floating down to Camelot, hanging in the hall outside his bedroom. The long poem was full of the things my father valued: romance, chivalry, honor. The Lady of Shalott had also chosen her own death.

But Lancelot mused a little space;
He said, "She has a lovely face;

God in his mercy lend her grace,
The Lady of Shalott."

On our way home, Jamie and I stopped again by our mother's grave, five minutes' walk from our father's. It was the way they always should have been: not husband and wife, buried side by side, but cordial neighbors, a five-minute walk apart.

It took us about a week to go through the contents of the house where we'd spent most of our lives. For that week Jamie and I slept in our childhood bedrooms, and walked the hallways where we used to slide in thick, fuzzy socks along the yellow pine floorboards.

In the attic, we sat cross-legged among stacks of cardboard boxes, sorting through history. The warm air smelled of wooden splinters. Beneath dusty lids, Jamie's old art projects sat beside my first short stories. In one box I found several of my baby teeth, along with all the letters I'd ever written to Santa Claus. In others, we unearthed handmade Christmas tree ornaments, our parents' wedding china, and sets of silver serving trays. Our twentysomething homes were too small to store a fraction of what we found. Jamie and his family lived in a tiny rented house, and I lived in one room. Still, we enjoyed the game of holding things up and asking each other, "What do you think this is?" and "Do you remember when . . . ?"

As children, we'd only occasionally ventured up the rickety steps that unfolded from a trapdoor in the ceiling of the upstairs hallway. The attic was chronically infested with roof rats, and baited traps lurked in the corners. Jamie and I sometimes heard the rats from our rooms at night, scurrying up the wisteria that clung to the front of the house.

"Do you have any nocturnal squirrels outside your window?" Jamie knocked on my door to ask me one night when we were seventeen and thirteen.

"Just a couple rats," I said.

"Well, yes." He grinned at me in his green terry-cloth robe. "That's what they are. I just didn't want to frighten you."

We found boxes of letters and half-full journals. Anything that bore our parents' handwriting felt precious. One box held fifteen years' worth of our mother's day planners, and even though they contained nothing more interesting than *lunch with Doug,* or *dentist 2 p.m.*, I couldn't help turning the pages and running my fingers over the marks her pen had made. I imagined carting the whole collection away with me, storing them for years, and someone else encountering them after my own death, and facing the question all over again of what to do with them. In the end, we left the planners where we'd found them. We couldn't throw them away, and we couldn't take them with us. The attic had held our memories for years, and without it, Jamie and I would have to learn how to hold them for each other. Our father's will, we discovered, had left the house entirely to his wife. Uncle Ward was the executor of his estate, and when he told me this I was briefly stunned. I'd loved that house like it was alive, and it was hard to believe that, after all these years, no part of it belonged to me. On the other hand, I knew I could never live there again.

We packed up the photo albums, the etchings by our grand-mother, and the paintings by our great-grandfather. We took the VHSs from the fireproof safe, so Jamie's wife could have them converted to DVDs. I took my father's childhood teddy, a large bear with thinning fur and a middle as hard as a bag of cement, who wore a plaid button-down and red shoes and was called Edward. We took the two chests. Shirlee told us we could leave anything we liked behind, and she would store it for us. But I felt an urgent need to identify what was precious, and to learn to let go of the rest.

In our father's office, I found a drawer containing all our high school report cards and certificates for school prizes, along with the programs for all my plays. I had no idea he had kept these things, and the drawer felt like an answer to some question I hadn't known I was asking. We left everything where it was, and closed it again.

Before I left to go back to school, David took me aside.

"Take care of yourself," he said. I was surprised and touched by the earnestness in his voice. "Get plenty of exercise," he advised, "that's the best way not to get depressed. I don't know how you get through something like this. If it was me"—he thought seriously for a moment—"I'd probably get married."

David hugged me. I think we both sensed we wouldn't see much of each other after that. All through our teenage years, we'd tried our best to pretend the other wasn't there. The tenuous threads that bound our vastly different lives together had broken, and we were finally free to let each other go. I wished him well.

Jamie and I packed up my Volvo and prepared to leave. We would return to the house several times after that, but it would never again be our home.

Jamie came back to Berkeley with me, and slept on the couch in my living room. Sally had flown home to their kids but encouraged him to linger. I'd thought of taking the semester off, but it was already paid for and I couldn't imagine what to do instead. My mother and father had left me enough money to finish college, and even to attend graduate school if I chose. I felt enormous gratitude. I knew another student who'd lost both her parents, and relied on funds set aside by the university to help her buy books and food. After graduating, there was nothing standing between her and the world.

I felt bad leaving Jamie alone all day while I went to class, but he assured me he didn't mind.

"Do you have any idea how happy I am to read and watch TV, and have no one ask me to feed them or clean up poop?" So I left him in my room.

I felt grateful to my professors for interrupting the thoughts that ran in a constant loop through my brain. Over and over, I imagined the rope, the tree, the feet dangling in midair.

In the evenings, Jamie and I watched *Firefly* on Netflix.

"It's space cowboys," he said, pitching me the first episode. "What's not to like?"

He stayed most of a week before returning to his family in North Carolina.

"You know," he said as he packed up his backpack to head to the airport, "you could always come live with us. I mean, if you ever wanted to."

He didn't look at me as he said it. He wasn't making a grand gesture, just stating a fact. I put my arms around him. It made no sense, of course—their house was barely big enough for the four of them. But I loved him for saying it, for letting me know I still belonged somewhere.

I finally joined the play rehearsals, several weeks late. The director had offered to recast me, but I was grateful to spend my evenings among other people. My role required an English accent, and the production hired a dialect coach to meet with me every few days under the buzzing fluorescent lights in the basement of Zellerbach Hall. I'd listened to English people speak my whole life, but the coach wanted a period dialect, something posher and more nasal than the way my father had talked. Every time I tried a line, I heard my father, and every time, the coach had to nudge me away from him. She spent hours gently coaxing me away from memory and into something new.

The play was a new script by Philip Kan Gotanda about the lives of Chang and Eng Bunker, the famous conjoined twins. I played an eccentric aristocratic lady who forms a friendship with the brothers in London and introduces them into British high society. The piece was still in development, and occasionally the playwright would stop to ask us, "What do you think you would say here? What do you think you would do?" Each evening I put on a corset and bustle and traveled back in time to 1830s London, where my whole life had yet to happen.

In 1874, Chang Bunker was the first of the twins to die. Eng Bunker remained connected to his lost brother for several hours before dying himself. *Yes,* I thought night after night, watching the play's final minutes from the dark wings, *that's what grief is like. Like there's another version of yourself that's been lost, but you keep carrying it around with you.*

After Jamie left, I began to dream my father was still alive. I would happen upon him in a bookstore, or a supermarket. At first I'd feel joy, then terrible guilt.

"Oh my god!" I'd say, my arms around his neck. "I've been telling everyone you're dead. Can you believe it? I'm so sorry! What a crazy thing to say."

Then I began to dream that I was with my father in the backyard. I took his hand and told him I understood that he was in pain. When I couldn't talk him out of ending his life, I would help him to do it, sometimes with a rope, sometimes with a knife. Because I didn't want him to be alone.

Antoinette came to Berkeley and took me out to dinner.

"It's so strange," I said, poking at a beet salad, "to think of him taking his life, after everything Mommy did to live. She fought so hard."

"And," she said, spearing one of my beets on her fork, "there's no reason to think that he did not fight just as valiantly as she did."

The tenth anniversary of my mother's death fell three weeks after my father died. I had no idea how to mark the day. She would not yet have been sixty.

In the attic's dusty boxes, I'd found a back issue of *People* magazine from 1975, carefully saved in a manila envelope. The magazine contained a three-page profile on my mother and a nonprofit she'd cofounded in Santa Cruz when she was twenty-three, providing free organic produce to senior citizens living in poverty. A large black-and-white photo showed her wearing an embroidered white tunic top and a low ponytail, and talking into an old rotary telephone. Only a year older than me, I'd thought, touching the picture. I knew my mother had done nonprofit and advocacy work before moving to DC, but I'd never understood the scope of it till now. I'd imagined small-scale community organizing, nothing that would garner national attention. Looking at the photograph, I again felt the collective weight of all those missed opportunities to ask her about herself. Her life on the page seemed so purposeful. I wondered if what my father and John had said when I was in Boston was true, whether I really did have her determination.

In the same envelope was a copy of *Mademoiselle* from 1977, which devoted several pages toward the back to "12 Terrific Women." My mother's picture was labeled *Kristina Mailliard, activist,* and sat beside *Meryl Streep, actress,* and *Ntozake Shange, playwright.* The glossy pages inside were like the entries in her datebooks, pinning her down in time, proving her existence. I wished every year of her life could have been documented in such clear and official detail.

My father's death had only deepened my hunger to explore my mother's history. Losing the second parent had severed something in me, and I felt rootless, adrift. I craved anything that could bind me to a context. After returning from her adventures in Europe, my mother had gone to college in Santa Cruz, where she would spend most of the next decade. There, she and her then boyfriend had started the nonprofit, which they named Grey Bears.

On the second page of the *People* article, a smaller photograph showed my mother kissing a tall man in his thirties with chin-length hair, a mustache, and a pair of belted khaki shorts. The caption observed that she and her cofounder were "putting their heads together" at headquarters. I recognized the man in the photograph. He'd come to our house one year around Christmastime, when my mother was very sick. He and I had played a game of basketball in the driveway. He had stood somehow apart from the many other people who regularly streamed through our house. I sensed then what is clearer to me now: the way a former lover always carries the contrails of an alternate reality in their wake, the ghost of the life not chosen.

In the years since breaking up with Zach, I'd been in two serious relationships. Despite the fear my mother expressed in the letter for my first period, that I would not feel worthy of love, both of these men had been kind and affectionate. She was right, however, in predicting that I would be drawn to older partners, just as she had been. I loved the settled feeling of dating someone with his own place, his own books, furniture, and garage. But, though I craved the safety and stability of these attachments, I also knew that I was not interested in marriage, and both relationships ultimately dissolved because there was nowhere for them to go. I had selected men who wanted commitment, then found myself unable to give it to them. In both cases, I felt I could see the life we would have together, stretching off into the future, but the future had always frightened me. Looking at the magazine, I thought about that other life my mother might have had. She might have married the man in the picture and stayed in Santa Cruz, and I would never have existed.

Ten days after the anniversary, I turned twenty-two.

From the chest, I unwrapped two southwestern shell bead necklaces. I flipped through the sketchbook until I found the place my mother had pasted their photographs, but the space beneath the pictures was blank. Somehow the entry had been skipped. For that year, the tenth without my mother, and the first without my father, there were no words at all.

Twenty-second birthday:

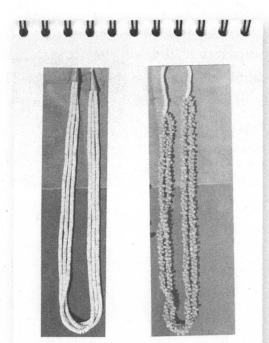

To celebrate my twenty-second, my mother's cousin Sandy and her friend Anne took me to spend the night at a gorgeous penthouse in San Francisco. The huge luxury apartment building stood at the top of Green Street in Russian Hill. The owners, family friends, were away for the weekend. Sandy, Anne, and I made a simple dinner in the magnificent, restaurant-quality kitchen, and sat in the little breakfast nook to eat. We stayed up late, drank pink champagne, and looked out the enormous windows, a 360-degree view of the city spreading beneath us.

Sandy gave me one of Granny Liz's etchings that she'd had for years titled *Young Cows on a Hill*. The black-and-white cows were arranged so that they seemed to flow into one another, and it was difficult to see where one creature ended and the next began. *A herd*, I thought, *of women*.

Late that night, all three of us got into one king-sized bed. Lying between them, I felt like a child again, crawling in between my parents after a nightmare. But a few hours later, I woke up in the middle of the night, alone. I called out in the dark, panicked. The room was excruciatingly hot. Out in the hall, I found the thermostat, but it was covered in so many buttons and dials I couldn't make sense of it. Farther down the hall, I found Sandy and Anne asleep, draped over bits of elegant furniture, as if someone had waved a wand and caused them to drop where they stood. In the morning, I learned that each of them had woken in the heat, tried and failed to work the thermostat, and sought the slightly cooler air of the living room. I found a love seat, and curled up near them.

The summer after my junior year, the UC Berkeley theater department offered a study abroad program at Trinity College in Dublin, Ireland. When the program had been announced in the fall semester, I'd wistfully imagined being the kind of person who jumped on a plane with a group of acquaintances to spend months on another continent. The week after I returned from my father's memorial, I went to the bulletin board outside the little wooden cabin that housed the Department of Theater, Dance, and Performance Studies, and wrote my name on the list.

I'd never expected to break free of my homesickness. I believed I would carry it with me, in one form or another, for the rest of my life. I had no memory of a time I wasn't preoccupied with place and proximity, constantly measuring the distance between myself and the people I loved.

But everything changed after David's phone call. My freedom did not come gradually, but in the space of one conversation. My fears, I realized, had not protected me, and so I gave them up. From that moment, I never again feared leaving. At first there was no joy in this freedom. The cost was too high. Like an animal who has bitten through a limb to escape a trap, I would need time to make peace with what had been lost, and appreciate what had been gained.

When I'd boarded the plane to Tufts, I'd felt I was leaving everything I knew and loved behind. When I stepped on the plane to

Ireland, I felt as though the distance scarcely mattered at all. Wherever I went, my father would still be gone.

I loved Dublin right away. It was the right height, the buildings tall enough to draw the eye upward but low enough to let in the sky. The eighteenth-century architecture of Trinity College enfolded me like a glorious stone cocoon, and each morning I woke up to a view of the bright-green, pocket-handkerchief lawn of New Square. My father's father had studied civil engineering at Trinity many decades earlier, the only one of seven children, in his family of Irish farmers, to go to university. The place held a tiny, weathered piece of my history, a fragment of the thread connecting my life to my father's and onward, back through time.

Our curriculum in Dublin was all plays: reading them, seeing them, staging them, writing about them. This intellectual diet seemed as decadent to me as the starchy meals and pints of Guinness I consumed daily in the local pubs. Ireland's connection to its own writers was like nothing I'd ever experienced. At the Irish theaters, the audience knew the plays by heart. I attended a production of Brian Friel's *Translations* at the Abbey (Ireland's national theater), and watched the people seated around me mouth the words along with the actors. It felt like being in church.

One wet night we saw a new play at a little theater somewhere in Temple Bar, and in the middle of act two there was a hanging. At the sight of the noose, my palms began to prick. As an actor approached the rope, I closed my eyes.

Afterward I stood in the alley outside the theater, waiting for the rest of my cohort to make their way out of the crowded lobby, letting the night air lower the temperature of my body. In the five months since my father's death, I'd noticed allusions to suicide everywhere—in books, movies, on social media—but they had not affected me this way. It was the image of the noose itself. With it came swarms of questions that I wanted to push away. My father's last moments, before and during the act, clamored at the edges of my conscious mind. I did not know whether my father had jumped off of something, or kicked it out from under him. I did not know to which tree he'd tied the rope. These questions had seemed difficult to ask in the immediate aftermath, and more impossible as time went by. The simple sight of a rope tied in a loop brought them all flooding into my brain. Knowing the answers, I felt, was the closest I could come to being with him while it happened.

The PhD student in charge of our group came outside to find me.

"What's up?" she asked, the yellow streetlights gleaming brassily off her short red hair. "Are you okay?"

"Yeah," I said. Then after a moment, "I can't do hangings."

"Oh, I'm so sorry," she said, "I didn't know."

"That's okay," I said, "neither did I."

My father's sister held a second memorial for my father in London, for those who hadn't been able to make the trip to California in January. Granddad was in his nineties by then, and found it difficult to fly. After my program at Trinity, I took the short flight to London and drove south to the small village where he lived. I found his house unaltered by the half decade since I'd last seen it. His immaculate lawn stretched away from the garden and down a steep incline to a row of trees at the bottom of the small valley. Until the last few years, he'd continued to mow it all himself with a manual push mower. He made us lunch and served it in the dining room with placemats and cloth napkins. He pulled a box of Eton mess from the freezer for dessert, and opened a bottle of champagne.

He looked so much like my father, sitting in the sunshine with his glass of bubbly. As the years went by, I imagined, my father would have grown to look more and more like the man sitting next to me. His hair would have thinned, and his hands would have spotted with age. He'd already worn glasses for reading, and by his nineties maybe he too would have worn them all the time. My father also loved champagne.

I tried to talk to him about Trinity, about the beautiful buildings, the sense of peace and tranquility I'd felt within its walls. I hoped Granddad would speak about his own time there, decades before, but he offered up few recollections. He was a taciturn man, classically English in his careful avoidance of emotional terrain. His time at university, I would learn later, had been complicated by undiagnosed dyslexia, insecurities about his rural education, and conflict with a jealous elder sister back home, who convinced their father to stop sending him money. I'd hoped my time in Dublin would forge a point of connection between us, but the city belonged to a part of my grandfather's life he'd been happy to forget.

Sitting there, I wanted something from him, some insight into what had happened. I struggled to put the questions into words.

"Were you very surprised when Daddy died?" I finally asked.

Granddad sat silently for a moment, looking toward some distant point on the tree line.

"Second marriages don't work," he said at last. And that was all.

Jamie's flight to London had been canceled at the last minute, so I gave the reading he had selected, the same one he'd delivered at our father's first memorial. He'd chosen a few lines from the end of J. R. R. Tolkien's *The Return of the King*.

> "Where are you going, Master?" cried Sam, though at last he understood what was happening.
>
> "To the Havens, Sam," said Frodo.
>
> "And I can't come."
>
> "No, Sam. Not yet anyway. . . . Your time may come. Do not be too sad, Sam. You cannot be always torn in two. You will have to be one and whole, for many years. You have so much to enjoy and to be, and to do."
>
> "But," said Sam, and tears started in his eyes, "I thought you were going to enjoy the Shire, too, for years and years, after all you have done."

"So I thought too, once. But I have been too deeply hurt, Sam. I tried to save the Shire, and it has been saved, but not for me. It must often be so, Sam, when things are in danger: someone has to give them up, lose them, so that others may keep them. But you are my heir: all that I had and might have had I leave to you. And also you have Rose, and Elanor. . . ."

Jamie had wept as he read it, thinking, I imagined, not only of himself but of his two small children, who would now grow up not knowing their grandfather. At the same time, the words seemed to contain a hope for what death might be like, finding a haven after a long, exhausting quest.

At the reception afterward, people asked me tactful questions. Some of them hadn't seen my father in ten years, or twenty, and they sought me out, just as I had sought out David, hoping that I would have answers. I had none. The details about the closure of the school seemed so flimsy and misleading that I hardly wanted to mention them. I knew my father had not killed himself because the school had closed. And yet, I also knew he had. To me, all their questions, and all of mine, boiled down to one overarching set of alternatives: Was his suicide avoidable, or was it inevitable? I did not know which answer was true, or which was better.

A year after my father's death, Shirlee called and asked to take me out to dinner for my twenty-third birthday. It had been many months since I'd been back to the house on McDonald Avenue. I wasn't sure what connected us anymore. Shirlee had a new boyfriend, and the two of them drove down to Berkeley to pick me up.

They arrived in my father's car. Through the window of my cloud-gray room, I watched the white Toyota pull into the drive-way. I didn't want to watch the two of them get out of the car, so I grabbed my coat and walked quickly out the front door before they could shut off the engine.

The boyfriend was driving. I slid into the back seat and arranged my skirt beneath me. We were going to a nice restaurant, so I had on my favorite dress. It was black, and printed with white origami cranes.

"Hello," we all said.

He backed out of the driveway, and drove along Stuart Street toward Shattuck. In the passenger seat, Shirlee reached out and placed her hand on the back of his headrest, just as she used to do when my father drove.

The gesture cracked something open inside me, and memories flooded in:

. . . My mother, father, Jamie, and I were all in the car on the way to see a concert. In the back seat, Jamie began twisting my arm behind my back; I shrieked.

"Gwenny, knock it off," called my mother from the front. She placed her hand on the back of my father's seat and turned to face me.

"But—" I began to protest.

"I don't care who started it!"

Jamie grinned at me. . . .

. . . My father, Jamie, and I were speeding along on the way to school.

"Full speed ahead, and damn the torpedoes!" my father yelled. The blue-and-red lights of a police car sprang to life behind us. . . .

. . . Shirlee, my father, and I were driving Tippy to the vet for the last time, her black-and-white head in my lap, her different-colored eyes half-closed. . . .

. . . Shirlee was driving and I was in the passenger seat, on the way to the cemetery, wearing a black skirt with a hole in the seam. . . .

Now a man I'd never seen before was driving, Shirlee was in the front seat, and I was in the back—all these years later—of the same car. I felt the sudden impulse to open my door at a red light and run out into traffic. But I stayed still, and stared at the paper cranes in my lap.

At the restaurant, we made polite conversation. The new boyfriend seemed like a nice, intelligent man, a person I would have liked if we'd met in any other context. I was glad Shirlee had someone new in her life. Maybe now we could begin to untangle our fraught connection, and I could let go of the resentful teenager I still sometimes became in her presence.

Once when I was sixteen, Shirlee had caught me sneaking handfuls of her expensive tinted shampoo. She'd said nothing at the time,

but later presented me with a bottle of my own. It had been a graceful, generous thing to do, and it made me want to find my own way
toward grace and generosity. I looked across the table at my father's
wife and her boyfriend, and thought they looked happy. After dinner they drove me home, and then the two of them got back into the
white car and drove away.

When I was ten, my father had given me a little red leather jewelry box, with different compartments for earrings, necklaces, and rings. It had a little insert that could be removed and packed in a suitcase. An engraved brass label on the top read: *Gwenny, with love.* By the morning of my college graduation, the red leather box had begun to grow crowded, my mother's gifts slowly occupying the velvet-covered spaces.

I much admired this ring, and your Daddy bought it for me. The original stone broke and I had it replaced. When my wedding ring

no longer fit me I often wore this as a wedding band. I've never tired of this ring nor found one I like better. I can't quite say why I like it so well. Taste is such a funny thing. Anyway, I hope you like it, too.
   XOX Mommy

I'd bought a new dress for graduation, large plum-colored circles scattered across a field of white silk. The ring I found inside the chest, a deep-purple amethyst flanked by tiny clear crystals, matched it perfectly. For many years, I'd thought I would never earn the right to open this particular box.

I slid the ring on, and imagined my father taking my hand after the graduation ceremony.

"Well done," he would say. That was what he always said, whether I'd won a prize at school, or fallen down and scraped my knee. "Well done."

I'd wait for him to recognize the ring. His own first wedding band had been a delicate braid of red, yellow, and white gold that looked as if it might be woven from wheat, or his own reddish-blond hair. After my mother's death he kept it in the top drawer of his bureau, and I sometimes took it out to look at it. I rolled it over and over in my fingers, looking for the join where the ends of the plaited strands must have been melted together, but the circle always remained perfect, eternal.

I would tell him what my mother had written, about how the stone had once broken and been replaced, and how she began to wear it like a wedding ring.

"Crikey," he'd say, "I'd forgotten about that."

And it wouldn't matter that he'd forgotten, because I'd have the pleasure of reminding him.

I gave the student address that afternoon before the families and friends of my cohort in the Department of Theater, Dance, and Performance Studies. My family took up an entire row of the theater: Jamie with Sally and their kids, my mother's siblings. Glancing down at them, I again had the impression of seeing my mother there, implied by the nearness of so many people who shared her blood. She never would have missed this moment, when I had finally done the thing she'd always known I could.

After graduation, I kept renting my room in Berkeley, while the other renters cycled in and out. I still felt lost and uncertain. I was twenty-three, with no parents to tell me what to do with my future. The freedom from any kind of external expectation was slightly exhilarating, and completely terrifying.

Once again I turned to the only thing I felt I truly knew how to do. With a few friends from college, I cofounded a small theater company in San Francisco. We had no money to option production rights, so our first season featured entirely new work by female writers, mostly our friends. For that season, I wrote and directed my first full-length play about three adult siblings who struggle to write their father's obituary after his suicide, as a tornado approaches their small town. The modest success of the production gained us a permanent residency within a slightly larger theater company, and I became the artistic director of our tiny organization.

I spent Christmas with Jamie and his family. The twins were five, full of energy and fun. They'd bought a new house in Charleston, South Carolina, and as the five of us sat around the (normal-sized) Christmas tree, I felt that it might be enough to belong to this family forever. Jamie's unexpected shortcut to fatherhood had offered me a home after I found myself without one, and while I would never cling to it the way I had clung to the house where I grew up, it was still a place to belong.

I flew back to California in time to spend the three days before New Year's with the Sensational Six at the house in Bodega. During that gathering, our fifth, someone suggested we all make up five-year predictions, and add them to our time capsule. I wrote that in five years I expected to be living in Ireland and writing plays. As I folded my scrap of paper, torn from a brown grocery bag, and added it to the jar, I realized that this was the first time I'd allowed myself to picture a future at all.

T wenty-fifth birthday:

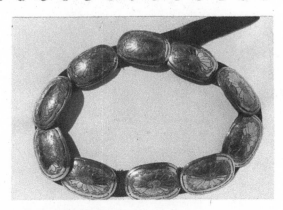

At one point during my rather unorthodox college career, I took time off to visit Indian reservations in the Southwest: Navajo, Hopi, Zuni, Santo Domingo. Each concho is signed by the artist. This has most likely become a collector's item.

On the plane to graduate school, I sat between Sandy and Anne, who had offered to deliver me safely to my new home in Providence, Rhode Island. They stayed with me several days and helped me find a little house to rent in Federal Hill, where the landlady promised them she'd watch out for me. They helped me unpack the suitcases I'd brought, while everything else I owned, including the cardboard chest, slowly crossed the country by truck. They took me to Target and bought me a cutting board, cleaning supplies, toilet paper. The three of us slept in a double room at the Holiday Inn, taking turns sharing a bed.

"Are you sure you'll be okay?" they asked as they packed the rental car to drive back to the airport.

"I'm fine," I said, and meant it. It had been seven years since my failed attempt to move east for college. Since then, every cell in my body had turned itself over. It might have happened to a different person.

My mother had also moved east for graduate school in her twenties, but she had gone to study business, and I was trying to become an actor. Some small part of me wondered whether she would have approved of such an unpredictable career, but another, larger, part of me felt certain that she would.

"You have a real knack for dialogue," she'd said when I was seven, after reading a short play I'd written for my friends to act out.

"Maybe you'll be an actor, or a writer." She'd said it as though these were perfectly reasonable things to be.

The small New England city was comforting in its proportions, a concentrated bubble in which to spend three years learning a craft. I memorized the walk from my front door to the theater downtown, and for a while I didn't need to learn how to go anywhere else. I learned the names of the other actors in my cohort, and they became the only names I needed, the ones that filled my mouth for ten hours a day, six days a week.

On my first night alone in a new city, I went to meet my classmates at a dive bar that on Mondays featured a sixteen-piece jazz orchestra. I turned from ordering a beer at the bar to see a tall man framed in the door. He had dark curly hair and mischievous hazel eyes. I'd noticed him five months earlier, when I'd attended the MFA program's Welcome Weekend for prospective students. Then I'd tried to stop noticing him, reminding myself that he was a potential classmate. The weekend had been a series of social events and workshops, during which I learned that his name was Will, that he was from Florida by way of New York, and that I very much liked his acting. On the second night, after a couple of beers, I'd leaned over to speak into his ear above the noise.

"So, do you think you'll come in the fall?" Some folks were still fielding offers from other institutions, making up their minds.

Will leaned toward me. "I will if you will," he'd said, grinning.

In the dive bar, jazz music swelling, I walked toward the figure in the doorway. He walked toward me.

"You came," I said.

"You came," he said, and we fitted our arms around each other.

Days later, Will asked me out for coffee. He said what we both knew, that there was obviously something between us.

"But we're here to learn," I protested, a rule follower still. "Everyone is. It's not fair for us to make this complicated."

He smiled at me across the wobbly metal café table. "I hear you," he said. "But I respectfully disagree."

When I stayed silent, he continued, "Look, let's check in about this again in a couple weeks."

Graduate school for actors, I discovered, was a lot like having your body and mind taken apart and then put back together. Before we could learn to act, we were told, we had to learn how to walk, how to speak, how to breathe. We practiced sitting in chairs for an hour without leaning against their backs to strengthen the muscles deep within our torsos. We practiced climbing stairs. We practiced standing still. We practiced saying our own names simply and un-apologetically. We practiced taking up space.

During the first week, after watching me play a scene, the movement teacher placed his fingers on my shoulder blades, gently drawing them together to broaden my chest, opening the space around my heart.

"So much more beautiful this way," he said. "We'll work on this for three years."

In speech class, we learned "American theater standard," a stage dialect that sounded like the accent of someone who'd grown up in the middle of the Atlantic Ocean.

In voice class, while I was speaking a monologue, the instructor pressed on my diaphragm and my legs turned to water beneath me, while more of it poured from my eyes.

"I don't know you yet," he said, "but you're holding something there. Do you have any idea what it might be?"

When my moving truck arrived, two weeks later than scheduled, several of my classmates helped me to unpack. They gamely moved furniture and held pictures level against the walls, in exchange for the beer and pizza I put out. Then they left, one by one, until Will and I were alone among the empty boxes. I forgot all my reservations as he kissed me in a pile of discarded bubble wrap.

I had no idea what had become of the cubic zirconia my father had planned to offer my suitors, but amidst the popping sounds of the bubble wrap, I still imagined Will carefully sorting among them.

Three months into my first year of graduate school, a stranger broke into my house. Will and I returned from a late night at the theater to find the back door slightly open. At first I didn't think to worry; I'd never been robbed before. Only when I got upstairs, and saw that someone had gone through my drawers and taken a pillowcase from my bed, did my mind lurch to the cardboard chest.

It sat at the foot of my bed, utterly exposed, a literal treasure chest in the center of the room. I stared at its laminated top. Something inside me was falling, and falling, and not hitting the bottom. I took a rapid mental inventory of all that was left inside: *twenty-sixth birthday, twenty-seventh, twenty-eighth, twenty-ninth, thirtieth, engagement, wedding, baby.* As I stood beside Will in the open doorway, the strongest feeling rising within me was shame. I hadn't yet told Will the story of the cardboard chest. The letters I had already opened were stored there too, and if they were gone, if I had lost them, I felt I could never tell him about any of it. How could I have left the chest so ill-defended? My whole body lit up with panic, but to let Will see my fear would be to admit the gravity of my mistake. It was like the coral necklace. If no one knew what I had lost, maybe the loss wouldn't be real. I bent down, as casually as I could, and lifted the lid.

Half a dozen packages and a handful of envelopes greeted me with their tidy labels. Not a single thing was missing. I offered up my silent thanks to the universe. Then I sat down on the bed, and when I had my breath back, I started to laugh. Will, still in the doorway, knitted his brows together sympathetically.

"I'm so sorry this happened," he said.

I waved his commiseration away, still giggling uncontrollably. "It doesn't matter," I said, and meant it. "It's fine."

The intruder had taken my laptop, an old iPod, and some jewelry from my dresser (nothing of my mother's). I felt indescribably lucky, as if I'd been given the gifts in the chest all over again. Afterward, when the police had come and gone, I placed the chest on a high shelf in the back of the closet and hid it behind a stack of blankets. I vowed to be more careful.

In spring, Will's parents came to visit and watch us in a student production of John Patrick Shanley's *Savage in Limbo*. I felt especially nervous, knowing they were in the audience.

"I've heard so much about you," I said to his mother after the show, shaking her hand. Then I looked down at the long red acrylic nails I'd put on for the character. "I just want you to know," I whispered into her ear, "these aren't my real fingernails."

"Okay," she said, and smiled.

I didn't know that our head acting teacher, Brian, who had sat next to her during the show and was acting in another play (dressed in drag), had just introduced himself and told her the same thing.

Will's parents took us out to lunch and asked me thoughtful questions about myself over plates of salad. I wished I could introduce Will to my parents. I felt their absence most keenly when someone new came into my life, and I realized that they would never get to know this part of me. I wanted to offer up a history, a context, wanted someone to pull out an album of baby photos at a restaurant. I wanted my parents and Will's to sit across from each other and compare the ages at which we'd spoken and walked and learned to read. We'd been born just four months apart, and our parents would have been around the same ages. They would have had so much to talk about. I thought how sweet it would feel to see the four of them gathered around a table, feeling each other out, making secret plans.

One night a few months after *Savage*, I told Will the story of the cardboard chest, and asked him if he would watch the video my mother had made for Jamie and me, which I hadn't seen since I was fourteen. I'd never shown it to anyone else before.

"It's going to be a lot," I said, "and you don't have to if it's too uncomfortable, but I think it could be a way for you to get to know her a little, and that would mean a lot to me."

Will didn't hesitate.

"I'd love that," he said.

We watched the DVD on my laptop, sitting on my bed. At first I kept glancing over at him, worried that he would become overwhelmed. But slowly the video drew me in, and I was watching and crying as I hadn't cried in years. Will put his arms around me, and I realized he was crying too. We watched until the end, and afterward we sat on the bed and pressed our wet faces together.

Just before the end of the semester, I got a phone call from Jamie. I knew something was wrong the moment I heard his voice.

"What is it?" I asked. I was standing in the lobby of one of the theaters, on break from rehearsing another play.

He told me his marriage was ending. I leaned against the wall and slid down it to sit on the plush red carpet.

"It's no one's fault," he said, "it's just the way it is."

I couldn't remember him ever sounding so low, so weighed down. I felt the sudden urge to smash something.

Enough, I wanted to say to God, or the universe. *Enough already.*

My sadness wasn't only for him. I'd spent every holiday with his family for four years. I loved going home to them, belonging to them. *Make a family*, my mind repeated to itself, *and the world will find a way to break it.*

"What will happen with the twins?" They'd just turned seven.

"We're going to split time equally. Sally found an apartment close by."

This, I realized, was what my parents would have done, if my mother had lived. They would have divorced and bought houses down the street from each other. They would have done everything they could not to disrupt our lives.

I hated to think of Jamie alone in his house, his children away with their mom. I wanted to jump on a plane and be in his living room by the time it got dark outside. I wanted to put my arms around him, put my body between him and the world. I wondered if he would keep the house. Home, to me, was wherever Jamie was. It had long ago ceased to be a physical place.

In my third year of grad school, I wrote another play about siblings grieving their parents' deaths. This one was about a brother and sister who mix their deceased parents' ashes together and drink them in a smoothie. The idea had been born from one of my mother's messages.

> *For some reason,* she'd said, *in our culture we have tried to banish death from our lives, and consequently we don't know very much about it. We don't have traditions that we can call on to help us. Each family has to try and figure out how to deal with it all by itself for the most part.*

Instead of casting their dead away, I wanted to find a way the siblings could bring them closer, as close as humanly possible, flesh inside of flesh. After doing some research, I realized I had not invented this idea. Similar rituals have been practiced in parts of Asia and South America. In the play, the point of the ritual was that the siblings came up with it together. It was not prescribed but spontaneous, and therefore authentic. I wondered if, had our father been cremated, Jamie and I would ever have done such a thing, if we would have found any comfort in taking inside ourselves some part of the body that had helped to make us.

· · ·

A few months before graduation, a friend from the directing program told me she was starting a theater company, and wanted to commission a play from me.

"But I'm an actor," I said.

"But you're a writer," she said, and she made it sound true.

T wenty-eighth birthday:

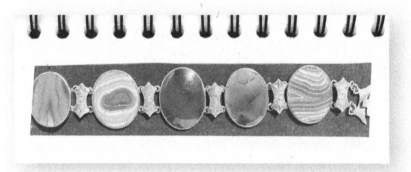

This bracelet came from your great-grandmother, Gwen. I thought it might appeal to the rock hound in you, my little Mineral Person.

I love you, Mommy

When I was a child, my mother was always quick to remind people that I was not named for my great-grandmother. She was Gwendoline, and I am Genevieve, but at some point, we each became Gwen. When I was growing up, a reproduction of a painting by my great-grandfather hung on the wall of our kitchen showing a young woman propped up in bed, reading. She wore a white nightgown, a pink silk dressing gown, and a long strand of pearls. A piece of gauzy pink material encircled her short, dark, flapper-style hair. The painting was titled *Gwen in Bed*.

Granny Liz's mother, a famously beautiful London socialite, was the villain of our family mythology. She had four husbands, and gained something different from each. Her first husband made her a young war widow. Her second, my great-grandfather, was an artist, and painted her many times. She left him, after eight years and three daughters, for a wealthy accountant with a knighthood, who died within a year, leaving her widowed (again) and rich. Her last husband gave her a son before he, too, died. In Gwendoline's hands, the story always suggested, marriage became a tool, a weapon.

When she divorced my great-grandfather, Gwendoline legally changed their daughters' last names, and refused to allow him to see them. Sometime after the day he gave Granny Liz the little chocolate man, my great-grandfather conspired with the girls' nanny to meet with them secretly in Regent's Park. He painted them, during the last of these stolen visits: three girls in bonnets and Mary Janes, the nanny sewing in the background, a double agent in hat and pinafore. Granny Liz would not see her father again until she was eighteen, just before she married and left England for good.

That marriage would also end in divorce. By the time she died, Granny Liz had married three times. My mother married just once, but, as I'd learned in her therapist's office, the marriage had been deeply unhappy, and had ended before she died.

Sometimes I pictured the four of us, my direct maternal line, each looking behind her to the woman who came before, searching for answers about how to make a life with someone. In my imagination we all wore little pith helmets, like Victorian archaeologists, and scrabbled among the debris of our pasts, wielding hard picks and gentle brushes, holding up our finds, one by one, to the light.

The agate bracelet was a thick cuff made from slices of pink and gray stone. It was a heavy, austere piece of jewelry. On my twenty-eighth birthday, Will and I were in our final months of grad school. In June we would move, along with most of our classmates, to New York and try to make our way in the theater world.

Over two and a half years, my connection with Will had deepened into something different from any relationship I'd ever known. In the past, I'd always assumed that my partnerships would end, that our lives would eventually go in different directions and we would let each other go. But now, for the first time, I had no concept of how this connection would play out. I felt completely, terrifyingly vulnerable.

One night, a few months after we began dating, I'd sat in Will's Providence apartment, drawing designs with my fingernail in the gray microfiber of his couch.

"I'm not sure I ever want to get married," I'd said, erasing one doodle with a brush of my hand and starting another. "I figured you should know in case that's important to you. I mean, I believe in relationships, I'm just not sure about the whole, you know, institution."

I waited a long moment while Will thought.

"I'm not sure about it either," he said, and we'd left it at that.

I'd set up this barrier between us, hoping it would protect me from losing something later on. If we never became a family, that family could not be broken. But I was learning, as the final weeks of grad school raced by, that Will and I were becoming a family, whether I meant us to or not.

We moved together, during the hottest part of summer, to a one-bedroom apartment in Brooklyn with big windows and a wall of exposed brick. We auditioned for plays and TV shows and commercials, and I tried to carve out quiet hours to write my play. It turned out that our new downstairs neighbor was a playwright, and she generously offered to read the script I was working on. I repaid her in sourdough bread made in my little gas oven, whose unpredictable igniter sometimes caused tiny explosions that rattled the cabinet doors.

When the movers had helped carry all our things up the two winding flights of stairs, I'd searched the closets for somewhere to put the cardboard chest. The chest was very light by then, with mostly air inside. The gifts I'd already opened fit neatly, if snugly, into my jewelry box, and I could easily have taken the remaining packages out and sent the empty chest to the curb for the recycling truck to pick up. Its corners had been slightly battered in the move across the country, and during another relocation someone had wrapped its body in clear packing tape to keep it closed. I hadn't been able to remove the tape without peeling off the laminated surface, so I'd simply used a knife to cut through the tape and free the lid. One of its latches was bent and wouldn't fasten. It was only cardboard, after all; it hadn't been constructed to take so much wear. But the container itself had become precious to me over the years. Its presence, even hidden out of sight in a closet, had kept my connection to my mother alive. For sixteen years, it had reassured me that the last conversation between my mother and me was not over. I tucked the mostly empty chest in the space beneath my hanging winter coats, and closed the closet door.

For my thirtieth birthday, Jamie came to visit us in New York, bringing his girlfriend. Anne was my age, with steady blue eyes and a mass of dark-blond curls. They'd been dating a few years, and it was clear she loved Jamie's children, who had just turned thirteen.

During their visit, Jamie and Anne slept on a blow-up mattress on our kitchen floor, and the four of us stayed up late into the night, playing cards and drinking beer at the pub across the street.

When Jamie and Will had first met I had prayed that they would like each other. I wasn't sure what I would do if the two most important people in my life didn't get along. I shouldn't have worried. The first time we all spent Christmas together, Jamie and Will got each other essentially the same gifts (a medieval-style earthenware beer mug, and a Viking drinking horn) without discussing it with me. Will and Anne had formed their own friendship, and were happy to spend time together while Jamie and I caught up.

"Can you believe it?" I asked Jamie, as we watched Will and Anne head off to the gym together.

"I know," he said. "Sometimes I feel like we're dating the same person."

Freesia had also flown in for my birthday, and on the night before, we all gathered in our narrow living room to count down the final minutes of my twenties. I was born at 12:07 a.m., seven minutes into my mother's birthday. At 12:06, I held out a thin rectangular leather case, tied with pink ribbon, for everyone to see. It had been twenty years since I'd opened the first gift from the cardboard chest with my mother beside me. Two decades later I felt the same thrill of anticipation. But there was another feeling too. The black sketchbook sat ready on the coffee table, its cover patinaed with use. This was the last birthday marked on the list that hung inside the chest's domed lid. To open it would be a new kind of goodbye.

"Ten, nine, eight . . ." we chanted, ". . . three, two, one!"

I pulled off the pink ribbon, and snapped it open.

Inside I found a beautiful silver bar pin set with sapphires, but when I flipped to its page in the sketchbook, the space beneath the photograph was blank. For the second time, my mother had left no information about the gift she'd chosen. Maybe she'd run out of time.

The first time I'd pulled a box from the chest, I'd believed my world would always be defined by the loss of my mother, limited to the few square miles her presence had infused with safety. For years, each subsequent package had felt like grasping at a tiny life raft on a dark, uncertain sea. But, standing in the living room of my own New York apartment, surrounded by people I loved, I realized my mother had already given me the tools I needed to make my way forward. She had gifted me permission to make my life larger, and richer than I had once believed possible. Still, I'd been looking forward to reading her words. Jamie, Anne, Freesia, and Will all put their arms around me as I stared into the bare white page, feeling the ending of it.

Thirtieth birthday:

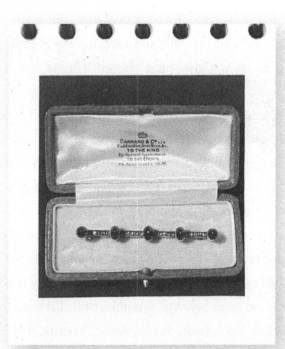

In our Brooklyn apartment, the little metal box with the braid of my mother's hair, cut the day we first shaved her head, lived on a little shelf above my desk. One day I found that moths had gotten into the box, chewing through strand after dark strand. Moth larvae, the internet informed me, feed on keratin, the structural protein found in natural fibers like cotton, wool, and human hair. I was startled to find that something had been living in the little box, which I associated so strongly with death; that the collection of inert cells could actually nourish something into being.

I took the braid into the bathroom and, for the first time in twenty years, undid the long thin plait, showering the white enamel of the sink with tiny razored fragments. I ran the warm tap, feeling oddly grateful to the moths for making it necessary for me to do this, for giving me once again, after so long, a sink-full of my mother's hair. I put the blow dryer on low, hoping not to lose too much of it in the breeze. The warm air brought back the hint of a smell I thought had gone long ago, a tiny whiff that wasn't quite my mother's scent, but was certainly something human. I noticed how few grays were in the dark bundle.

As I laid it out on the dish towel, I thought back to a time when I was very little, and my parents still bathed me in the evenings. My father would lay a big pink towel down on the tiled floor, before scooping me from the cooling water. He'd place me in the center of the towel, and I'd curl myself into a little naked comma. He would fold the edges over me and tuck in the corners, then pick up the whole bundle in his arms.

"A pink package!" my mother would exclaim as he set me down on the bed beside her. "What could be inside?"

I'd giggle from inside the terry cloth. She'd unwrap me slowly, peeling back one corner at a time.

"A foot! I don't remember ordering one of these. An elbow! My goodness, what could it be?"

Finally, after I was completely revealed, "It's a Gwenny! What a great package."

Night after night my father presented me to her, and night after night she was delighted to discover me. It became my favorite game. *We'll have to get a bigger towel*, I thought, *for when I grow up*.

I rebraided the lock of hair and put it back in the box (this time in protective plastic). There was less than before, but it was clean and cared for, and somehow more mine.

In the wake of my thirtieth birthday, three packages still huddled together in the bottom of the cardboard chest. The first was a hexagonal black container printed with bright-red berries and labeled: *Engagement*. The next was a Celestial Seasonings tea tin with a picture of a bear wearing a nightcap. Its little white note card said: *Wedding*. The last, a tiny cardboard box: *First Baby*.

My mother and I used to play a game that she always won.

"I love you more! No, I love you more!" she and I would repeat back and forth to each other, like a chant, like a dare.

"No. I love you more," she would always end by placing her two hands on the sides of my face, "and you will never know how much, until you have a child of your own."

I heard this as both a promise and a prophecy: that one day, by having children, I would know true love, and it would be greater than the love I felt for her. I could not conceive of a bigger love than I felt for my mother, but I trusted her when she said it was possible.

The little cardboard box marked *First Baby* fit easily in the center of my palm, no larger than a walnut. Its pink ribbon was tightly knotted, keeping it closed. To get it open, I'd have to use scissors, to sever something permanently. The packages marked *Engagement* and *First Baby* also came with thick envelopes, their weight promising a wealth of fresh words.

In all the years I'd had the chest, I'd never been tempted to open a package early.

"You must have amazing self-control," people often said to me, when I told them about the letters. "I'd have opened them all years ago."

Self-control has never been one of my strengths. Neither has patience. But I did grow up reading myths and fairy tales, and I knew what happened to people who were too curious or greedy and ignored instructions. If I were reading the story of my life, it would be obvious that the little girl whose mother left her a box full of gifts was meant to open them one by one, at the right moments. If she didn't, I would expect something terrible to happen to her. If she did everything perfectly, there might be a reward, beyond the contents of the gifts. Her mother might even be returned to her. These things happen in fairy tales. For more than half my life I'd followed the instructions, and now I was nearly at the end of the story. For all those years, the final three boxes had formed a distant horizon. Glimpsed from far away, they seemed to promise understanding, a new intimacy between my mother and me. I imagined that when (and if) I opened them, we would finally meet as equals, peers—wives and mothers. But what if I didn't choose those things? What if my life took me somewhere else?

The ribbon tied around the packages had grown creased and

faded. I wondered, looking at them lined in the bottom of the chest, whether any daughter can help but pattern her life on her mother's, either in imitation or in reaction. I thought of other young women, all over the country, the world, on the phone with their mothers, fielding questions about relationships, marriage, and grandchildren. If my mother were alive, wouldn't she be another one of those mothers asking loaded questions at the other end of a video call? Wasn't this simply another version of the same thing? It was. And it wasn't.

I chose a night when Will was away at the theater. The envelope marked *Engagement* closed with a button-and-string fastener, so there was no seal to break. I carried the bulky letter to the couch, the same gray microfiber one from Will's graduate school apartment where I'd sat to tell him, a few months into our relationship, that I never wanted to get married. It had been five years since then, and even though I still worried that, for me, marriage might be a doomed proposition, I'd also never loved someone this way before. I wanted to talk to my mother about him. I wanted to lie on her bed with her hands in my hair, and this seemed like the closest thing.

The string unspooled in slow spirals, and I imagined her hands winding it up more than twenty years before, moving clockwise to my counter. Like the letter for my first period, it was typed, and dated from the summer of 1996, the first time her doctors gave her a year to live. There was no audio recording, but I found that I could hear her voice in my head just the same.

My Dearest Little Gwenny,

Of course you aren't so little as you read this, but you are little as I write. You are only seven years old and I am facing the terrible sadness that you will be growing up without me.

I want so fervently and with all of my being to be with you for all of the important, and unimportant, things. I want to be here with you to love and protect you, shield you and encourage you, help you see and know all that is best in you, and help you work on the stuff that gets in the way of your happiness.

But you have weathered the storms, found your own bearings and are ready to commit to a lifelong relationship. I can't begin to imagine all that has happened to you along the way. All this seems so far in the future, twenty years? Who can know.

Please, I hope, I pray that you have learned to love yourself enough, to feel yourself worthy enough, to have chosen someone who can really love you and honor you.

A true marriage is a marriage of what is most sacred in both of you. In a true marriage, partners hold each other's souls with the greatest of tenderness and respect and support one another in the quest, the search, the yearning for what is most sacred in this life.

If you do not recognize and commit to that divine spark in each other, then it all comes down to the logistics, accumulations, and to-ings and fro-ings and the doings of life.

Your father and I were not able to commit to the sacred in each other. Yet, we are both good people; responsible, dutiful, and devoted to you and Jamie.

My greatest wish, besides being able to grow old and be here for you, would be to have given you and Jamie a happier marriage in which to grow up and develop your ideals and expectations.

Perhaps, Daddy has remarried and has found a happier relationship in which he feels more grounded and less discontented, and has been able to provide you with a better model of what marriage can be.

I feel deep regret at my inability to give myself, and you, a more loving, vibrant, and harmonious marriage. And, we will never know if we all would have been better off if Daddy and I had tried to start anew with someone else using all of our hard-won experience to guide us. Because we were so devoted to you and Jamie we couldn't bear to hurt you by breaking up your home and instead we hurt you by not being able to truly come together with trust and kindness, and devotion to one another's soul.

How does one come to know how to weigh and balance, truly reckon the trade-offs and consequences?

Daddy and I had such a difficult time because we had not learned to love ourselves just for being ourselves as children. We were both so insecure about our value and worthiness that we kept looking to each other to provide validation and took completely to heart even the most subtle suggestions of criticism. We both stored up so many hurts and grievances and disappointments that an insurmountable barrier rose up between us. You can't find your worthiness in another person. You must know and value yourself first. Despite the fact that Daddy and I can see and appreciate fine qualities in each other we seem to have lost the way to trust and goodwill. The patterns have been established and even in the face of my premature death we cannot seem to break out of them. I tell you this because I want you to know how important it is to be truly ready to enter a life partnership. And the best way to be ready is to truly know yourself and love yourself.

It is my deepest hope that our great love for you has given you what you needed to choose wisely and happily for yourself, and that you have come to know in your truest place that you deserve to be cherished and that you in turn will have the capacity to cherish your partner. What one cherishes isn't about competence, or successfulness or physical attributes. It is about seeing our best self reflected in the other's eyes; our most loving and sacred self—not their notion of what should be, but supporting what is already ours through the divine spark that gives us life—and that we hold the same concern for them. It is about having the freedom to give expression to the light we each carry within us while joining our life force with another's for mutual support and comfort. This kind of love takes a lot of maturity and hard work but even that isn't enough if the person is not grounded in themselves to begin with. One must have an ease about both giving and receiving, a capacity for forgiveness for oneself as well as for the other, a kind of loving detachment that allows one a sense of perspective, and a willingness to take responsibility for one's own stuff, which we all have no matter how squared away we think we are. We must have our own internal wellspring of well-being to draw upon.

My darling girl, I wish you the greatest of happiness and long life together. There is a certain kind of growth and maturity that only comes with the kind of commitment you are making, just as there is a certain kind of love that only comes with raising children. It isn't for everyone but I am glad to think it might be for you.

I love you, dearest Gwenny, with all of my heart. How I wish I could be with you, hugging and crying and beaming with you. I cry thinking about my quicksilver sprite all grown up into a beautiful woman about to wed her life to another's. I don't know why the joy of sharing this must be taken from us. Why sharing the joys and sorrows of all that has come before must be taken from us as well. I am trying so hard to make some kind of peace with myself. You can't imagine the anguish with which I write these letters for you. I feel such despair for the mistakes I have made and continue to make knowing there's no time to make them up to you. I am still learning how to be a good mother to you. You are such a unique and complicated little creature and need such firm and tender care to help you discover who you are and why you are here.

Gwenny, I am so sorry to be leaving you. Please forgive me. Please let the love I feel for you find its way to you. I know a box of letters and tokens can't begin to take my place or make up for my loss to you. But I wanted so badly to do something to ease your way through the future.

May God bless this union you are making with your beloved. May it bring you the greatest joy.

Your loving Mommy

I let the tears flow. No matter how many of my mother's messages I read, they always reduced me to sobs. They seemed to touch some chamber of my heart usually walled off.

I went to my bookcase and pulled out my parents' wedding album, a thick blue leather-bound volume. From its pages, my parents smiled up at me, my mother in ivory silk with puffed sleeves, my father in a white bow tie and tails. It was the kind of wedding girls are taught to dream of, with beautiful clothes, important guests, and elaborate floral arrangements. They were twenty-nine and thirty-one when they married. At thirty, I sat directly between them.

I was grateful that my mother's letter had acknowledged problems in her relationship with my father. But despite the turmoil of her own marriage, there was an optimism behind the pages in my hand. She still hoped that I might love differently, better. The letter even hinted at her own longing for a second chance at love. Again and again her letters had begged me not to close myself off from love, not to allow her loss to keep me from letting people in, from risking intimacy.

I ran my eyes again over the advice she offered: *One must have an ease about both giving and receiving . . . a kind of loving detachment. . . . We must have our own internal wellspring of well-being to draw upon.* Married or not, I figured it was something worth striving for.

When Will came home, I hugged him and pushed the letter into his hands.

"Will you read this?" I asked.

Gwen and Will, engaged 4/30/23.

AUTHOR'S NOTE

One February afternoon, while making final edits to this book, I stumbled upon an unmarked green folder tied with a black ribbon. The folder contained a thin stack of my mother's letters I'd never seen before. They were addressed to my brother and me, but, unlike the letters in the cardboard chest, they were not marked for specific occasions. Instead, they were dated like journal entries, written during the years between her terminal diagnosis and the destruction of her sight. I was stunned. Not only did they provide me with new insights into my mother's thoughts, they also offered an invaluable corroboration of the timeline I'd been trying so hard to reconstruct from old photographs, web searches, and interviews with family and friends.

The experience of researching and writing this book has been full of moments like this one, impossible gifts suddenly dropped in my lap without explanation. Committing this story to paper has been like trying to take hold of something ever-expanding. Each time I believe I've found the last of my mother's secret clues—her hidden envelopes, boxes, and instructions—I'm proven wrong. When I look again, there is always more.

Two years into this project, I reached out to one of my mother's old boyfriends (the one from her European travels), whom she'd dated in her late teens. I emailed him on a Sunday afternoon, and four hours later I had a response.

Gwen—

Yes, I'd love to talk to you about one of my favorite people. Before she died she asked me if I would be a resource of information/memories/understanding for her children—so it has come around.

Reading his email, I felt the same rush of excitement I'd felt at nineteen when my mother's therapist said the same thing, the thrill of being on the right track. Both moments came with a sense of something growing larger, and a new appreciation for the breadth of my mother's preparations, the way they brimmed over the cardboard edges of my chest and spilled out into the world. I often wonder if there are more people out there, still waiting for their phones to ring.

One letter in the stack did belong inside the cardboard chest. My mother wrote it for whichever birthday turned out to be my first without her. I should have opened it the morning I turned twelve. It went missing for twenty-two years, but found its way to me in the end; another reminder that the story my mother has been telling me all these years, about her, about myself, is not over yet.

My Darlingest Gwenny,

This is your first birthday without me. I don't know which birthday it is that you are celebrating, or how long it is since I have been gone. I am fighting as hard and with as much love as I know how so that this first birthday without me is as far into the future as I can make it.

At this moment I am writing, you are a delightful seven-and-a-half-year-old. I love your brightness and quickness. I love your beautiful elfin face and long graceful body. I know the fierceness and determination that sometimes get you into trouble now will

*one day come to serve you well. I want to be there to help you
learn how to make them serve you.*

*Because we share a birthday, this first birthday without me
may be especially difficult. You may feel guilty that you are here
when I am gone. Please know that I want you to have a long
happy life more than anything else I can wish for. You deserve
a wonderful, bountiful life full of love and joy. And sharing a
birthday will be such a special way for you to remember me and
feel my boundless love for you.*

*Love is stronger than death. I will always be part of you. I love
you, love you, love you with all my being—forever and ever.*

Love, Mommy

ACKNOWLEDGMENTS

I have been blessed with many fairy godmothers in my life, but never expected to find two in my beloved agent, Brettne Bloom, and brilliant editor, Marysue Rucci. Together they shaped and guided these pages, always steering me toward the deeper, truer places I could not yet see. I am forever grateful for their patience, compassion, bolstering, and discernment.

Before I wrote this story down I lived it, and that would have been impossible without my lifelong ally and big brother, Jamie Kingston, whose wit, humor, and affection offered me courage when I was out. Deep gratitude to him and to our wonderful extended family for their invaluable memories, insights, and fact-checking.

Thank you to Zeynep Özakat for listening to the first rambling outline of this story on a park bench, and assuring me that it was a book. To Dan Jones and Miya Lee at *New York Times* Modern Love for publishing the essay that would become the book. To Emily Rapp Black and Blaise Allysen Kearsley for their keen eyes on my earliest sections, and to Jessica Ciencin Henriquez, Adam Dalva, and Kathleen Tolan for helping me weave together the final threads.

Huge appreciation to the Bousa family, who offered me the priceless gift of time and space to write. To my dear friend Freesia Stein, who read the manuscript at every stage and tirelessly cheered me on. And finally, to my partner, Will Turner, whose commitment to art and artistry continually inspires me, and whose love, patience, and support make everything possible.

Kristina Mailliard
February 17, 1952–February 7, 2001